VIOLENT
LEADERSHIP

VIOLENT
LEADERSHIP

BE A FORCE FOR CHANGE

Disrupt. Innovate. *Energize*.

WESLEY MIDDLETON

ForbesBooks

Published by ForbesBooks, Charleston, South Carolina.
Member of Advantage Media Group.

ForbesBooks is a registered trademark, and the ForbesBooks colophon is a trademark of Forbes Media, LLC.

Printed in the United States of America.

10 9 8 7 6 5 4 3 2 1

ISBN: 978-1-94663-318-7
LCCN: 2017956640

Cover design by George Stevens.
Layout design by Megan Elger.

This publication is designed to provide accurate and authoritative information in regard to the subject matter covered. It is sold with the understanding that the publisher is not engaged in rendering legal, accounting, or other professional services. If legal advice or other expert assistance is required, the services of a competent professional person should be sought.

Advantage Media Group is proud to be a part of the Tree Neutral® program. Tree Neutral offsets the number of trees consumed in the production and printing of this book by taking proactive steps such as planting trees in direct proportion to the number of trees used to print books. To learn more about Tree Neutral, please visit **www.treeneutral.com.**

Since 1917, the Forbes mission has remained constant. Global Champions of Entrepreneurial Capitalism. ForbesBooks exists to further that aim by bringing the Stories, Passion, and Knowledge of top thought leaders to the forefront. ForbesBooks brings you The Best in Business. To be considered for publication, please visit **www.forbesbooks.com.**

To my wife, partner, and friend, Alane.
Without her selfless support and persistent pressure to be better than
I really am, this book would have never happened. She has always
demanded my best, and while this was uncomfortable at times, she has
been a force in molding me into who I am today.

To my children—Hayleigh, Austin, and Colton.
Seeing you live the things we have taught you and seeing the decisions
you are making affirms that this style of leadership is effective.

TABLE OF CONTENTS

CREATING A COOL CULTURE

FOREWORD

Violent Leadership . . . shocking words in this soft, easily offended culture; but Wesley Middleton challenges our thoughts and ideas without apology. *Violent Leadership* is not the typical how-to book about business but rather a clear roadmap that takes the reader to the destinations of change.

Wesley places into the hands of the reader the sharpened tools of proven methods that slice through the cords of corporate mediocrity. *Violent Leadership* leads you through the quagmire of culture change and lifts you to the firm footing of tried and proven success. If you intend to continue walking the worn path of comfort and safety, this book might not be for you. If you enjoy being rocked in the cradle of contentment, there are other books to quell your quest for the best; however, if you are looking for a ladder where each rung takes you high above the status quo, you have chosen the right book.

Wesley gets what many others do not. He takes the preconceived ideas about business and shakes them until you are liberated from the confines of the usual. I watched Wesley emerge triumphantly after trudging through the archaic ideas of other entrepreneurs and becoming an inspiration to me and many others. Early on, when we met to discuss the launching of his new company, I saw a spark that would ignite a transformational revolution in the business world.

I've known Wesley for many years and have had the privilege of observing him as a loving husband, father, businessman, servant, and friend. Wesley loves God, his family, and others while leading a company destined for higher heights. He has balanced the heavenly and the earthly while venturing into uncharted business territory and willingly sharing his wealth of knowledge and experience.

Every reader will not apply the principles in this book, but those who dare to step out of the norm will undoubtedly leave the comfort of the contented crowd and be lifted to lofty destinations.

Do you have the courage to read these pages and live them to affect real change? If the changes seem daunting, remember you are not required to do everything, but now is the time to do something. Let's get started and lead!

—**Ron Macey, Senior Pastor, Royalwood Church**

ACKNOWLEDGMENTS

God is the ultimate source of my strength and inspiration. Without faith in Him, I would not have followed His direction. The realization of my personal goals and dreams for an organization that exemplifies teamwork, Violent Leadership, and transparency is only made possible by my two partners, Stan Raines and James Zapata. This is not one man's story but one that is not possible without the hard work, dedication, and sometimes difficult conversations that we have had. You have both been unselfish and patient. Stan, without your ultimatum and push, who knows what would have happened. It was that moment that Violent Leadership became your style and we were thrust into the great organization that we have become. James, your constant and calm demeanor, along with your true desire to always be better and learn, has rounded out our team. This is truly *our* vision for MRZ.

My parents, Fred and Barbara Middleton, for the life and business experiences that you gave me at such a young age. You allowed me to fail miserably at times, but you were always there to support me, pray for me, and encourage me.

My pastor and mentor, Rev. Ron Macey, your model of calmness, emotional control, and execution of unpopular decisions have been textbook examples of great leadership. You have had an invaluable influence on my life.

My friends at Wolters Kluwer who have believed in me and allowed me the platform to tell the MRZ story; Samantha Grovenstien-Deal, Brien Siet, and Heffy Provost, you guys are incredible inspirations and so supportive of my thoughts and ideas.

Evan Tierce, our practice growth partner and my personal sounding board for crazy ideas, thank you for listening and offering reason while allowing me to be me in our strategy sessions.

Catherine Seitz, for the hours you have spent on this project. Your writing skills are unmatched. Your candor and passion for MRZ is evident.

Jon Meadows, my business partner, for every time you walked down to my office just to tell me something very positive and express your appreciation for the direction of MRZ. Those moments came at times that I needed them most for encouragement.

Bill Reeb, for your counsel and affirmation of greatness that could be, thank you. You have no idea the influence you have had on my career.

A WORD FROM THE AUTHOR

When I participate in various leadership groups or similar meetings, the conversation invariably comes around to leadership style, teamwork, and sources of information. People often ask each other, "What do you read or follow as inspiration? What books have you read lately?" I try to read some of the more popular books, and in these pages I will reference several of them as deep dives into specific areas. These authors have influenced my leadership style and helped to mold me into who I am today; I have gleaned an immeasurable amount of information from them.

Beyond books, there are two primary sources of influence and inspiration for me, affecting every decision I make. One of the most interesting sources of inspiration for me is professional sports, specifically the NFL, one of the most results-driven, success-by-leadership, and team-first organizations that exists. The brand management and laser focus of the NFL is spot on, and the organization is a great example of change management and team play information. However, "What have you done for me lately?" is a common question in the NFL and very relevant to today's business community.

Even two Super Bowls does not guarantee you the position of head coach for life. Just ask Tom Coughlin—now there is a leader who brought discipline, respect, and credibility to an organization in dire need, but when he was unable to deliver, he was expendable. Coach after coach, leader after leader, and CEO after CEO have been dismissed, despite an incredible record of success, for one reason: What have they done *lately*? You simply cannot expect your past successes to guarantee your future. Change and evolution is imperative for sustainable success. And yet, I have encountered many organizations that have people in leadership positions who are resting on their laurels.

The second main source of influence and inspiration for me is Rev. Ron Macey, my pastor and mentor. I have watched Pastor Macey stare conflict and turmoil in the eye and remain constant in his decisions. The changes he initiated at Royalwood Church were unprecedented. Not only were his decisions unpopular with some, they were costly. The dark days that followed many of the decisions would have caused a weaker man to change course and bend to popular opinion. I watched him maintain a positive outlook and retain his composure when, inside, he must have struggled with forces of doubt and lack of faith. No one would have known this. Unwavering and strong, he battled personal health issues, attacks on his family, and the backlash from unpopular decisions. He pressed on and led us to the place of his vision. His leadership transformed a traditional congregation to one of purpose, an incredible example of leadership and change management.

VIOLENT LEADERSHIP: A DEFINITION

The phrase "Violent Leadership" is not something you would expect to see in the business world, yet it refers to a distinctive type of leadership that is passionate, innovative, and disruptive and above all takes things by force. It does not refer to fighting, anger, or brutality. It is a positive and energetic pursuit of purpose and success. We discuss this more in chapter 1.

Matthew 11:12 (KJV) reads, "The kingdom of heaven suffereth violence and the violent take it by force." The Modern English version says, "The kingdom of heaven is forcefully advanced, and the strong take it by force." I live by those incredible words: violence as force and as leadership.

Violent Leadership has been my style of leadership from day one. It has evolved and grown, been tempered and threatened with termination, but it is still at the core of my belief that goals and success do not just happen. Achievement takes planning, action, risk, and disruption—it takes Violent Leadership.

In business leadership, you can see this force as an intense focus and pressure from your competitors. Can you see this ferocity around you in your profession? It is violent. It is not killing and looting, but it is an aggressive, zealously disruptive pursuit of goals. Your world is disrupted by the determination and wherewithal of your competitors. It is disrupted by technological advances, political policy, and generational differences. Professional services, specifically the accounting profession, are certainly not impervious.

This turbulent and disruptive environment demands Violent Leaders. A Violent Leader does not wait for change and disruption to determine success but strives with the utmost eagerness and effort to attain the privilege of leadership. Violent Leadership requires action, assertiveness, and a proactive style—a style that takes risks and leads the change within an organization, whether that is a business, family, church, or other organization. It demands a leader who will make tough and sometimes unpopular decisions and yet persevere. A Violent Leader knows what he or she wants and takes it by force.

Howard Rambin, cofounder of Moody Rambin Interests, signs his emails with this statement: "Success comes by doing things." It is that simple. In the following chapters, we will see how this is a core tenet of Violent Leadership.

HOW YOU WILL BENEFIT FROM THIS BOOK

This book will help you regardless of your status in middle-market America. It will help you whether you are a partner or are about to make partner, whether you are an emerging leader or an owner of a privately held business, and whether you are a pastor of a church or a professional service provider who is running your own company, such as a financial planner, doctor, lawyer, engineer, accountant, or architect. This book is for the professional service company that no longer wants to be held captive by traditional ways of doing business and wants to expand and grow in the twenty-first century.

It will also appeal to you if you are part of the up-and-coming generation and want to be successful in professional service companies. It will speak to your particular needs, culture, and expectations. It is also relevant to those of you hiring this generation and will help you listen to them, adapt to them, and attract them.

While speaking to large audiences about the state of our industry, I have introduced the concept of Violent Leadership and found a huge demand from people wanting to learn how to implement this philosophy in their own business. Clearly, it is time to challenge the status quo.

In professional services, I have seen companies cemented in their ways, neither willing to change nor seeing the opportunity for change. There is a need to shake things up and do things differently, not for the sake of being different but because our future demands it. This is not about reinventing the wheel and not about taking unmeasured risks. In the following pages, I introduce you to changes that worked elsewhere in an industry that has been resistant to change. I show you how I implemented technical innovation, made abstract concepts tangible, and breathed passion and originality into a traditional industry with remarkable success. Having implemented this philosophy myself, I know it produces results.

Chapter 1 explores the concept of Violent Leadership in your workplace. It looks at the dynamic of Violent Leadership, where strength and violence is not an outward demonstration but an internal attitude and drive.

Chapter 2 looks at two key ingredients in Violent Leadership—disruption and change—and asks the central question: Are you just changing the rules or are you changing the game?

Chapter 3 explores the willingness to fail and why this is an essential part if you are to implement and make progress as a Violent Leader.

Chapter 4 investigates the idea of being a thermostat or a thermometer—that is, are you setting the temperature or the tone of your firm, or are you riding the status quo?

Chapter 5 looks at how to assign roles as a Violent Leader according to your strengths. This chapter focuses mainly on the partners and owners of your firm and explores who should be wearing what hat.

Chapter 6 explores the idea that it takes all sorts to make a village. It explores the effective repurposing of responsibilities that was introduced in chapter 5 but takes them companywide and proposes a new model to replace the outmoded professional services model that is currently followed in most firms.

Chapter 7 looks at a central theme in Violent Leadership—how to create a cool culture that fosters loyalty, high performance, and retention in your firm.

Chapter 8 takes a hard look at personal housekeeping—how you can get in your own way and what you need to be willing to do to get out of your way and out of the way of your firm.

Finally, **chapter 9** explores the disruption caused by the millennial generation and how you can harness this to make your firm successful.

This book not only will help you implement a leadership style to create success, but it also offers practical, real-life examples from my experience implementing this style. I share my own successes and failures so that you can learn from the failures, emulate the successes, and blaze a trail in your profession as I am doing in mine.

Take what you learn in these pages and become a positive disruption, a positive force for change and success. Seek to attain your goals with passion, strength, and force, not by being passive but by being proactive. Take risks; be the disruption that allows you to achieve your goals. Take your life and your business in hand by force. Do not follow, lead. Operate with a confidence that is dynamic but generous, strong but not chaotic. Pursue your goals violently! Be more passionate and forceful than anyone around you. Be a force to be reckoned with. Be a Violent Leader.

CHAPTER 1

VIOLENT LEADERSHIP

VIOLENT LEADERSHIP MIGHT SEEM like an unusual title, but on closer inspection it encapsulates the momentum and vision necessary for effective leadership today.

It may surprise you that the inspiration for the concept of Violent Leadership came from scripture. When I look at those words on the page, even when I hear them in church, I interpret them as being active—taking the bull by the horns, seizing opportunities, and not waiting for someone else to make decisions.

I am an entrepreneur because I did not want a company deciding my future. I wanted to be in control of my own success. To achieve that, I needed to make things happen, often by force. Rarely does anything happen by happenstance. We achieve because we stir the pot and harness the creative energy that produces positive force. We are the agents for this force and momentum coming into being.

WHAT IS VIOLENT LEADERSHIP?

Violent Leadership originates from the King James version of Matthew 11:12: "The kingdom of heaven suffereth violence and the violent take it by force." In this scripture, *Thayer's Greek Lexicon* defines "violent" as "those who strive to obtain its [the kingdom of heaven] privileges with the utmost eagerness and effort."[1] *Strong's Concordance* defines "violent" as "a forceful, violent man; one who is eager in pursuit."[2] The HELPS Word studies further defines it as "positive assertiveness."[3]

"Violence" has a positive context in the original Greek word *biazó*[4] or *biaios*,[5] which is translated as the laying hold of something with positive aggressiveness. It is a positive, energetic, eager effort to effect change. In Latin, "violence" comes from the word *violentus*, which is equated with strength, robust energy, and enthusiasm.

Merriam Webster defines "violent" as "marked by the use of usually harmful or destructive physical force" or "extremely powerful and forceful and capable of causing damage." In my philosophy, it means the powerful energy that is capable of causing change.

In this book, Violent Leadership refers to the ancient meaning of the word. In the business arena, it refers to momentum, positive philosophy, and change or displacement that comes about through aggressive action, not passivity.

1　http://www.bible-discovery.com/dictionary-license-thayer.php
2　http://www.eliyah.com/lexicon.html
3　http://thediscoverybible.com/features/word-studies/
4　http://biblehub.com/greek/971.htm
5　http://www.biblestudytools.com/lexicons/greek/nas/biazo.html

THE EMERGENCE OF VIOLENT LEADERSHIP: MY STORY

My philosophy of Violent Leadership, and indeed the very existence of Middleton Raines + Zapata LLP (MRZ), came after a long journey filled with hard lessons, optimism and disappointment, promises, and limitations. MRZ is an example of a firm that came into being as a result of its partners being stifled at other firms. I got tired of thinking, "I'm sitting here at a firm with ideas and a strategy to grow, develop, and be a leader, but it is not happening. I'm pushing. I'm prodding. It is just not happening." I came to the conclusion that nothing would happen unless I took hold of the situation.

I grew up around entrepreneurship. My dad owned shoe and clothing stores, so I was exposed to the realities of running a business from day one. This gave me great experience on top of the business development type of mind-set I naturally had. I am a builder, and I wanted to build stuff. At eighteen, I went into the Air Force Reserve, and when I got out I went to college to learn accounting. I graduated, got married, and started making my way in the CPA world in a small town in Mississippi, population two thousand.

I had learned a lot in my time managing one of my dad's stores, as I did from my studies in college and my day job as a fledgling CPA. But the biggest and hardest lesson I learned was not from those early successes but from my greatest failure at that point in life.

It started as a great idea. What if we delivered pizza and videos at the same time? I acquired a small video store and a pizza restaurant. Because I had a job as a CPA, I hired a manager to manage the stores and restaurant. It was a good idea for its time; we ran a video store that delivered videos and pizza at a time when video stores were a big deal. We opened several locations, and while it started out as a very successful enterprise, it was not long before it turned into a spectacular failure.

While I was at work at my day job, employees made cash deals with customers to avoid having to pay the distributor its share of the video rental revenue. They thought they were helping, but the vendor discovered the practice and said it was a violation of the contract—which it was. What is more, as I started paying a lot more attention to the business, I realized we owed money to everyone. We were ruined.

It was a tough lesson. I learned later that the failure of that business was a failure to assess risk correctly, particularly financial risks. I learned a lot about assessing risk at that point, after I had already taken more risks than I should have. By not being intimately involved in the business, I had allowed financial resources to be over-extended—we had guaranteed credit purchases that we could not have repaid if we had been asked to.

I also learned that you cannot just offload the responsibility of running a business to someone you pay to manage it. You need to watch the details, or you need to hire someone competent to do that for you.

Another lesson regarded disruption or change in industry. We were trying to grow and develop in an industry that technology was about to decimate. Look at Blockbuster. From that venture, I learned to anticipate change and look ahead. I now anticipate the disruption or even destruction of a business through technology because twenty years ago I did not anticipate that videos and even DVDs would go the way of the dinosaur. But someone knew. Look at Netflix today. People were talking about it, but I wasn't listening.

After our disastrous venture into business ownership, I gathered my wife, Alane, and two children, Hayleigh and Austin, quit my job, and moved to Houston. I had to start over professionally and with my marriage. It was an incredibly dark, hard place. I felt like a complete idiot. I had failed on all fronts. The great vision I'd had starting out had gone horribly wrong, due to poor management, failure to anticipate change, and failure to hire and monitor the workings of the business. I had failed my family and put their future at risk. It is a difficult story to tell, because it's painful, but I have come to own it because that experience helped make me what I am today. As hard as they are, we often learn more from our failures.

Looking back, Alane should have cut bait and run. Any other woman would have done so for less reason. But part of my story is her story, too. Early in our marriage, she was the one who pressed me to finish college and take the CPA exam, and now it was her strength and drive that made me get back on my feet when our business failed. She patiently searched the Internet for jobs in Houston. She called recruiters, emailed firms, and set up interviews for me at CPA firms. Failure was not an option for her.

I was feeling pretty beat down as she was trying to build me up. I knew I had to be more aggressive. I knew I had to take control of my career and say, "I am going to make this happen." I had a renewed drive to prove myself to the world. I had a chip on my shoulder that drove me to prove that I was not a failure and that I knew what I was talking about. This was when the idea of Violent Leadership started to evolve. It meant you don't stop: You keep going back to the well. You get up every morning. You put one foot in front of the other. You keep believing in what you are doing. You keep believing in the values and principles that you know are within yourself despite circumstances suggesting that you did things wrong. That was all I could do—work hard and be the best I could be.

I had learned that you can put ideas out there, but the execution does not happen just because you did so. It takes a hands-on approach, and that was how I determined I would approach business from then on. My experience in the video store had taught me the difference between leading, delegating, and being hands-off.

In 2000, our family made the move to Houston, where I eventually landed at a firm (let's call it Jones & Smith) as a tax principal. My career was off to a great start and I had so much to learn. There at Jones & Smith, I grew professionally and technically and truly learned how to develop relationships. I recognized the fire that I had within me to be an advisor, a builder, and an entrepreneur. I could no longer imagine a situation where I would want to be anywhere else.

It was a great job. I was a partner. I impacted the firm. I helped influence the direction. I was financially successful. But something was not quite right. It was like a firm comprising ten separate organizations sharing a name. I wanted a team of ten partners pulling the wagon all the same direction. I began to learn the value of teamwork. I learned to question whether I had partners I was aligned with or whether we were sharing a name but fighting for resources. I also recognized my passion for leadership and realized I would never fulfill that at Jones & Smith.

I had to make a choice: either move to a new firm or take the team I had built and start my own firm. It was time to do some serious risk assessment. It had only been a few years since the video store in Mississippi, and I was scared of risking everything again. Besides, I had young kids, and I was responsible for my team of five or six people. I was not ready to assume a risk of that magnitude for me or for them. Moving to another firm was the safer bet and settled better with me at that time. We wouldn't have to worry about the startup costs. We would have a soft landing and financial security. I went for the safer bet. In 2009, Stan Raines, the team, and I moved to the tax department in another Houston firm (let's call it MillerBrown).

When I say tax department, they didn't actually have one. I was brought in to create it. I was told I could build it my way, which was very attractive to me.

They handed me the keys to the car, so to speak, and said, "Here—this tax department is your car. Go drive it. We're not going to mess with you." They were true to their word. They stayed out of the way and let me manage the situation. They knew it was a disaster of a department. They had failed repeatedly trying to get it off the ground. They needed what we had desperately.

In the first couple of years, the department became exactly what it was supposed to be. Stan Raines, our new partner James Zapata, and I built the department as a team, our way. Within ninety days, we took a terribly disorganized, unprofitable, failing tax department and turned it around. It became organized, profitable, and technically savvy, and it started attracting new clients. We brought $1.5 million in business with us, and from there the department grew to $2.5 million in the first year.

It was everything that we said it would be. We rebranded the firm, changing the logo, the name, and the website. I kept reminding MillerBrown of where we needed to go. They saw all of this positive change and were impressed.

My partners at MillerBrown saw that I had a business development and growth mentality, energy, and a vision for the future. A couple of years into our time at MillerBrown, the partners approached me and asked me to lead the firm. I accepted the role. They needed new blood, but when it came time to take more steps into marketing and business growth, I ran into a headwind of resistance. I couldn't get them to buy into my ideas.

I advocated inbound marketing. For our purposes, inbound marketing involved developing website content to drive prospects to us based on their search for solutions to their needs. Producing the content required the experts—the partners—to write and develop content. I knew it could work for CPAs just like every other industry. But the partners' first response was generally "That will not work." I would ask, "How do you know it will not work?" They had a typical CPA mind-set—highly risk averse. Most CPA firms don't believe that what works for any other industry would work for them.

As much as they needed change, they were not willing to let someone else lead. They did not believe in the strategy I proposed for growing the firm in terms of client relationships. They just could not buy into doing things differently. It took me a while to discover that their progressive intentions were hobbled by a poor governance system. Any change I wanted to implement was not going to happen.

MillerBrown had hit its ceiling—it would never realize its potential, because the partners would never let anybody lead it to a better place. With the firm stuck at being every man for himself, with every decision based on "What is best for me?" no one made a decision based on what was best for the organization. They had a feeling of belonging, but there was constant turmoil at the executive level because there was no vision for the firm, no five-year plan, no sense of direction, and no sense of purpose.

This experience further honed my Violent Leadership philosophy. I recognized that a firm that does not allow itself to be managed or led is exactly what I did not want. An effective organization needs to start with the guy at the top being willing to give up control. A leader who forces majority ownership just to have control is not a leader.

It struck me that this was the second time I had tried to implement a change in vision at a conservative CPA firm and found it did not work. I could only go so far before banging my head as I tried to convince the partners to believe in my vision. Finally, Stan Raines, who had been with me since 2001 at Jones & Smith and had also watched things unfold at MillerBrown, sat down in front of me and said, "Wesley, you and I have been together a long time. You hired me. I would never hurt you, but on December 31st, I am leaving this firm. I cannot stay here. I'm done with it. We've talked about this before, and either we can do what we've talked about or we can go somewhere else and do something different."

The lights came on for me. I resolved to take my vision and do something with it. It was time to really implement the philosophy of Violent Leadership that Stan and I shared. I had been trying to convince MillerBrown of the right path and they were not listening, but I was like a dog with a bone. With Stan's prompting, I realized I was being aggressive in the wrong fight. I needed to muster the courage to go out on my own again.

I learned long ago that my success would come because I made it happen, not because anyone handed it to me. I knew I needed to charge ahead in a positive and energetic way and do what I could to get people to follow me. I had been doing it for other people's firms; now it was time to do it for my own.

Four years later, in 2013, Stan Raines, James Zapata, and I launched our own firm, Middleton Raines + Zapata, with a team of eighteen.

What MRZ has allowed me to do is unleash the energy, innovation, and change inherent in the concept of Violent Leadership. The success of this application of force became quickly apparent in our metrics. Between 2013, when we started, and 2017, we grew from eighteen people to almost a hundred. We grew from about $2.3 million to over $13 million in annual revenue. We went from one office to three. For two consecutive years, the *Houston Business*

Journal named us the number-one place to work in Houston based on our employee feedback. We have been among the top five fastest growing CPA firms in the nation since our inception, according to *Inside Public Accounting* (IPA), a leading profession publication.

VIOLENT LEADERSHIP IN PRACTICE

People's response when I tell them about my Violent Leadership style is to open their eyes in surprise and ask, "What the heck is that?" I have learned that the concept takes some explanation—not just a definition but a view of how Violent Leadership actually looks in the workplace. If nothing else, this opens the door for discussion of our style of getting things done, our innovation and willingness to change, and our search for ideas and improvement.

Part of that style is not fearing the outcome of change and being okay with a potential failure. We have learned to say, "Hey, we are going to accept some failures along the way, knowing that to attain success, we are going to have a few no's." This means being willing to take a chance on an idea that a trusted member of the team proposes even if I do not understand it, and vice versa. This attitude has promoted a culture of innovation and collaboration. In some ways, violent culture consumes everything—it is like a tidal wave that pushes everything in its path.

Amanda Shook, our employee experience officer, came to me and said, "We say that we promote family and good health and welfare, so I'd like to buy chairs that have an exercise ball." I could not see it, but I told her, "Get ten of them, and let's see what happens." That is a small example of someone who had an idea that fit our culture and the willingness to try it.

Our client experience officer, Kevynn Brewer, wanted to measure the satisfaction of our clients and recommended that we implement the Net Promoter Score system. As a result, we send out regular Net Promoter Score surveys. The survey's single question is "On a scale of 0 to 10, how likely are you to recommend this company's product or service to a friend or a colleague?" Based on that feedback, our client relationship managers are empowered to promptly fix a problem if they find one, no matter how small. Kevynn responds to every single concern that comes up, which gives our clients a sense that they matter and are heard. It reflects our style of taking ownership and active leadership in everything that happens.

A walk through our office offers a clear example of our leadership style. The energy in the office is striking. This comes in part from our employees knowing they matter, that they are heard, and that their ideas are taken on board. Our seating arrangement is also open. There are no cubicles, only open, collaborative areas, which we call pods. This fosters open communication and collaboration. The partners walk around and talk to people. We interact with each other. We will stop with somebody who has been with us for a couple of days and have a conversation with them. It is common to see interaction at all levels.

Unlike most accounting firms, you will see a lot of meetings in partners' offices, people coming together in different places. We're very collaborative. We have found that we all come up with ideas and solutions better if we sit down and talk about them, if we collaborate on them—not just sit at our desks with our heads down, focused on work. The result is a more solution-focused culture.

Not all meetings are to discuss problems. Our tagline is *Ideas, Answers, and Results*, and this means we have meetings to generate new ideas and new approaches. Our culture revolves around ideas and solutions for our clients. Clients are looking for solutions to challenges, hurdles they face in their business and channels. We are here to solve those. One process we use is to pick a client who needs a solution and then get in a room and brainstorm: "What is this client facing? What challenges? How do we help this client?" We will spend an hour focused on that client so that we can come out of the room with ideas that we can give back. The client will get a call, "Hey, we were sitting around talking about you, and we've got four or five things we'd like to talk to you about."

We generally choose these clients for brainstorming sessions based on their revenue size, but sometimes a client relationship manager will know a client has a crisis going on or an event coming up, such as a business transaction, death, marriage, or divorce, and will propose that we get together and think of solutions. Lifestyle events are not really our problem, but it improves business and client relationships when we try to be an incubator for helpful ideas and planning.

Sometimes a client will come to us and say, "Hey, I have (a kid going to college, a divorce, a marriage) coming up. Can we meet?" We then get everybody in the room. We have whiteboards in most offices, so we can brainstorm and draw out solutions for them.

TWO KEYS TO ADOPTING VIOLENT LEADERSHIP IN YOUR BUSINESS

Be willing to listen

To implement a Violent Leadership style in your business, you can start at the top by making sure partners are listening to staff. It is important to create a culture that says, "We are listening."

You need partners to be out in the space interacting with staff at every level, listening to them and getting ideas. Not everything will be implemented, but the act of listening is key to encouraging staff to think innovatively and communicate ideas, and it gives them a feeling of belonging and a sense that they have some influence in the firm.

The effectiveness of our approach shows in the awards we have received (see Appendix A for a complete list). These show that people here feel like they are an integral part of this firm, and this benefits our bottom line. We have low staff turnover, so we don't incur the cost of hiring and retraining people. There is an indirect benefit in having happy people who are plugged into a culture they want to be part of. It is more than just a job—they get to be part of what is going on.

Growth in the bottom line is another indirect result. There is no question that we grow because we serve our clients well and because we have a service model based on ideas and a results-based culture. Our revenue has shown fivefold growth since we started out. We are becoming more efficient. With our metric, which we call "realization," we have found that we are able to realize 10 percent more per hour because people are more efficient. We believe our huge gains in efficiency come from our high staff retention: happy people being retained results in high efficiency.

Be willing to change

We all say we are willing to change, but Violent Leadership means recognizing if you are willing to be the change agent. You have to lead the change. You have to make the first step so that everybody will follow you. If you don't change at the top, nothing will change, because there is no one to follow.

FINAL WORDS

Listen to the people around you. The youth who are coming up are a force to be reckoned with and agents for change. Listen to them. Take one idea and implement it, and be willing to fail. It is okay.

Stop settling for the status quo and believing that somehow you are immune to the technology or other disruptions that are prevalent in our economy today.

Those who are complacent will not see the force that is coming, but if you are reading this book, you are not one of them. You are clearly interested in knowing how you can be better. Keep doing that. Keep searching for ways to improve and be better, because that will give you a competitive advantage.

CHAPTER 2

THE COURAGE TO CHANGE

ONCE UPON A TIME there was a firm of introvert accountants who loved numbers, dwelt in the past, and rarely saw the light of day. Those days are no more.

When I decided to leave MillerBrown, I was making a decision about how I wanted my life to be. I could stay there making a great salary and being okay, or I could make a change and do the things I wanted to do. That meant uprooting my entire team, taking a risk, and walking out the door to launch a new firm.

That is not everybody's first choice, and I am not encouraging everyone to quit their job and start their own company, but that decision took more courage than anything I have ever done. It felt like I was stepping out and taking everybody's life and livelihood into my own hands. The question then was: "Do I believe enough in myself to step out there and say, 'Here's how we're going to go do it'?"

That first real change was probably the most difficult, but there were three other significant changes that had to be made and took a lot of courage.

UNDERSTANDING POWER

One of the greatest dynamics of Violent Leadership is the role of submission and having the heart of a servant. Submission occurs when I open myself up to the criticism of the team around me, take that criticism to heart, and examine myself. Understanding power means owning the humbleness of the trust placed in your hands and recognizing that your service to others trumps all else. It means admitting you are not perfect, which is difficult when you are an overachiever. It means owning your flaws and working on them rather than hiding them for fear of appearing weak. Violent Leadership does not just exist in the world out there—it exists in your inner world, too, where you need to accept criticism and make changes, often painful ones, in order to grow and allow the company to grow.

A question that I asked myself once we set up MRZ was: "Do we have the right people in the right jobs?" Our profession forces CPAs to be salespeople, although I have seen other professional organizations take the smartest and most technical revenue generators and make them salespeople. Why not hire salespeople to sell and let the CPAs deal with accounting and advising? The number-one reason I have found that CPAs do not do this is that it erodes the power base of the partner in charge. The partner in charge ceases to be the rainmaker, because sales growth can happen without them.

In most professional service firms, the person developing the business holds the power, and everybody depends on them to bring in new business. That person is the rainmaker. At our nascent firm,

I had the power of the rainmaker, and I used it to make my second major decision—to give it up. I knew that CPAs weren't good sales-people, so to grow our firm I needed to admit that it could not depend on me. We needed to create a machine or a system that created new business. Since changing the business development model means letting go of power, it takes a lot of courage to say, "Okay. I'll give that up for the greater good, which is to build a system that develops business that isn't relying on any one person."

Putting others first, doing what is best for the team even though it comes at great personal cost, and keeping the anger and defensive response in check—these are all dynamics necessary to be a Violent Leader. This is a very hard place to be. It needs the Violent Leadership style to proactively keep emotions in check and maintain composure when faced with strong criticism. This is not an easy lesson to learn, but it's an important one. Violent Leadership is not only about how we lead others—it is also about how we discipline ourselves as leaders.

RISKING INNOVATION

At one point at MRZ, we were wasting a lot of time tracking every-body's time off and arguing every year about how much to carry over. Do we lose it? Do we get it? Do we pay you for it or not pay you for it? Is somebody sick?

If people need or want to take time off, we believed that they are going to find a way to do that, even if it means lying about it.

This led to the second change to streamline our human resources: not tracking time off or vacation time. We allowed people to take as much time off as they wanted. Instead of micromanaging them, we told them how many hours they had to work. We decided to stop telling people what they could not do and instead said, "We need this many billable hours from you. You focus on that, and we won't worry about the rest of it." In order to get their billable hours in, they had to act like adults, be accountable, and tell us when they were going to be gone and when they were working remotely.

We had a situation where the son-in-law of one of our longtime employees was diagnosed with cancer. Our employee needed three months off to take care of him and his family, but she did not have three months' vacation. It felt very negative to say, "No, you cannot have any more time off." Instead, we focused on the positive. In that scenario, we told her we would not worry about it, that she could go take care of her family and we would figure out how to get her hours in later. In the end, she came up short by the numbers but was so grateful for this flexibility and understanding that we simply agreed to forgive the excess time off as her bonus for the year. Did we benefit economically? Not in a measurable way, but we stayed true to our values and supported her and her family. We benefited by having an employee who would be forever loyal to the firm.

We still have the HR system where everybody requests time off, but it is more like an accountability system than a regulatory one. Of course, March 15th until April 15th is a blackout period. Let's face it, this is a CPA firm—no one can take a vacation then. We need everyone to buckle down during tax season, but once April 15th arrives, they can take the summer off. Unless we see a problem brewing, as long as they do what they are supposed to do and clients aren't neglected, we don't care. Actually, it helps us, and it helps their work–life balance.

It was a scary leap to make. Once announced, I was concerned about whether anyone would show up the next day. Luckily, they did. It took courage to step out and be the first firm to do this. We have tweaked it since its inception, but overall it has been terrifically successful. People love it—not only because of the flexibility it gives them but also because it shows that we trust them to do that right thing. That is part of our Violent Leadership culture.

MANAGING RETENTION

Our approach to human resources has been a great contributor to our high retention rates. In fact, unlike much of the professional services industry, retention is not one of our challenges, for a number of reasons: our openness and transparency, our vision, and our passion. Any lack in these areas is a reason for people to leave.

If you have a retention problem, look at three aspects of your business.

First, does your firm stink—literally? If you haven't painted or refurnished since 1972, if your infrastructure is a shambles, and the office is dark and dank rather than open and transparent, it is time for a makeover.

Second, do you lack vision? Does your team have any sense of purpose or common goals? You need to inspire your team with a shared vision. You need to identify and define your values, especially if you are to inspire the millennial generation, whose careers are generally energized by companies with purpose.

Third, do you lack passion and energy?

If these aspects are true of your firm, it's time get up and get moving. It's time to adopt Violent Leadership.

CHANGE THE GAME, NOT THE RULES

Another significant change we made in the organization came about when I handed out the book *The Apple Experience*,[6] in which Carmine Gallo presents Apple's five steps of service that all customer-facing employees follow to engage customers in a retail setting: Approach, Probe, Present, Listen, End with a fond farewell.

Sometimes the best ideas and best practices are not in your organization or even in your industry. They are outside. When looking at the client service experience, the best ideas are generally not found in CPA firms. Instead, they come from the Four Seasons or the Ritz-Carlton or Apple. The Apple experience was a good fit for us because it focused on innovation.

Our team needed to look outside of traditional CPA systems and processes at other CPA firms. We needed to create an experience akin to someone walking into an Apple Store and being greeted by a genius who knew exactly what to say and how to say it. The Apple experience is an experience, not just a chance to buy a new phone. That is what we wanted: a true experience, not just an opportunity to pick up your tax return.

The MRZ experience was inspired by Apple. We wanted to create a true client experience, not just "Here's your tax return." We wanted to emulate Apple, to create a team of geniuses, which we called client relationship managers (CRM).

Repurposing Traditional Roles

Most firms have an executive assistant who handles administrative tasks. We decided to repurpose the executive assistant role from a purely administrative role to a true client interaction role, the CRM.

---

6   Carmine Gallo, *The Apple Experience* (New York: McGraw-Hill, 2012).

It was an example of Violent Leadership, saying, "I'm going to do this. I'm going be the guinea pig. I'm going to demonstrate how this works. If it fails, it fails. If it does not, it does not. We will see."

We hired our first CRM, Blanca, who has a degree in sociology and had client service experience at another professional services firm. I said, "Look, there's an administrative part of this role, but we want you to be the client-facing relationship manager, where you understand how to be nice to clients and proactively get them to the right place. We CPAs just don't know how to do it."

Blanca is now the epicenter of the client service experience. The other partners saw the difference it made and decided to shift their own executive assistant's role to follow suit. Now we have six CRMs. They don't sit out in front of a partner's office like in most firms, just taking care of that partner. Instead, they sit together in one area, in a pod, because their focus is the client experience, not the partner. They feed off each other and help each other. If one has a problem, another jumps in. They are empowered to solve problems, and they know exactly what to say and how to say it. Their number-one purpose and goal is to serve our clients.

Many other firms that have heard about this structure want to adopt it, but it is not necessarily easy to do. You must hire the right person. You cannot turn your existing executive assistant into a CRM if he or she does not have the skill set for it. The courage to change demands that you be willing to let go of someone who does not fit what you need in order to replace them with someone who will. Sometimes you have to cut some people loose to make room for those who fit what you are trying to do. This is not always pretty.

Today, we go outside our industry to get regular client service relationship training. We have developed our own client service manual to help our CRMs know exactly what to say within our processes, and we have someone on our team who is a great CRM lead the training process.

We also introduced the role of client experience officer, responsible for everything related to our client experience. We just implemented the Net Promoter Score (NPS)[7] based on the recommendation of Kevynn Brewer, our client experience officer. The Net Promoter Score is tracked for every partner, and we adjust, respond, and correct based on our feedback. Of course, asking for feedback can be painful. Sometimes you don't want to look at yourself and hear what people say about you, but at the same time, the NPS makes people accountable. It makes it possible to address anything that might not be working the way it should. What we are finding now is that we are getting back some very good scores, which tells us we are doing the right things.

UNIQUE BRANDING AND PURPOSEFUL GROWTH

I tend to have many original ideas, although I am aware that originality does not necessarily mean an idea is good. One idea I knew was good was my notion for growing the practice—and it didn't involve trying to turn CPAs into salespeople, as most firms are wont to do. It was an approach to sales and marketing that involved an accountable, focused effort. It advocated the right people for the right role, which means leaving CPAs to be good CPAs and installing a business development team with the right skill set for sales. First, we outsourced the cold calling. We use Salesforce to understand our customers better through their personal preferences, to solve problems faster

---

7   Net Promoter Score is an index ranging from −100 to 100 that measures the willingness of customers to recommend a company's products or services to others. It is used as a proxy for gauging the customer's overall satisfaction with a company's product or service and the customer's loyalty to the brand.

by accessing past customer interactions, and to identify new sales opportunities by analyzing our best customers' histories. Our sales team focuses on developing new leads and new relationships and only brings the partner in to close the deal. Then, in our onboarding process, the business development team hands off to our CRM.

When it comes to marketing, CPA firms have historically treated marketing people as party planners. Our philosophy of Violent Leadership meant taking action and being innovative, so this led us down a different path. We didn't look at what other CPAs were doing; we looked outside and asked, "Okay, what are real leaders doing in these areas?"

Evan Tierce, our practice growth partner, and Catherine Seitz, our brand experience officer, led us to use inbound marketing, which relies on solid writing and content marketing. We built our website in HubSpot, which at the time was the cutting edge in content curation (the gathering of information relevant to a particular topic or area of interest), inbound marketing, and lead development. This also gives us a highly ranked website—not because we rely on Adwords but because our inbound process is driven by statistics, just like our business development.

We had come a long way from our days at MillerBrown when I proposed the strategy they rejected, which we later rolled out at MRZ. We hired an in-house marketing director and outside consultant. We developed individual marketing plans. We spent time and money targeting our audience, our markets, our industries, and our clients, and devised plans to attack them.

Thankfully, there is a more mature space for inbound marketing today. Inbound marketing was a little more cutting edge three years ago and certainly was radical for the CPA profession, which could not understand the point of having everyone writing content and giving away our intellectual knowledge on the Internet. However, other industries were proving that this was attracting people. We needed to not be scared of sharing knowledge. It drew people in and made us experts, but that was hard for traditional CPAs to understand.

Today, we are a top-ranked CPA website. As a result, our traffic is incredible. The leads we get from people reading our content are high quality, because when they contact us they already know we are the experts. My expertise is in oil and gas. Some of my blogs have been top ranked by Google from organic search. We did not have to pay for search engine optimization (SEO) for that to happen.

Our strategies worked. It was crazy in our profession to think that someone with no training as a CPA could actually go out into the marketplace and sell our services. It was crazy that we should not have sales goals as CPAs and that the various business associations would be better represented by someone other than a CPA who really did not want to go to the meeting anyway. It was crazy that focused cold calling would actually work in our profession. It was crazy, but it worked. An enormous part of our success as a firm has been the implementation of this wild and crazy idea that a CPA firm could grow in the same manner and with the same tools and processes as any other business.

THE DESIRE TO BE GREAT

One of the phrases you will hear in our offices is "being good is not good enough." Here, we want people who want to be great at what they do, and we believe this greatness takes innovation. It takes something extra.

We encourage our people to be great at something. We are all great at different things. If you are not focused on being great, you are going to be mediocre. Violent Leadership does not accept mediocrity. If people feel it is okay to be mediocre, then they will not last here. They need to move on to somewhere else.

The Violent Leader never accepts the status quo and does not accept that just because something was one way last year it should be the same way this year.

TAKE THE FIRST STEP

It is important to step out and do something daring, something new. Someone has to take the first step. When you step out, you are stepping into the unknown, and you have to be willing to be the guy who steps out with an idea and finds that it doesn't work. To achieve, paradoxically, you need a willingness to fail, a subject we will look at in more detail in the next chapter.

FINAL WORDS

Find one process in your firm that is more client centric and have the courage to implement it. Client-centric thinking leads to success.

Stop asking people to do jobs that require skills and strengths or expertise they do not have. Putting the wrong people in the wrong roles is a mistake. You should not expect your team to be successful if the skills demanded for the role are not their strength.

CHAPTER 3

THE WILLINGNESS TO FAIL

WHEN WAS THE LAST time you made a decision that was outside an acceptable norm in your profession or your business?

When I look back at the early days of our firm, we made many decisions that were fraught with risk. One seems like a small decision today, but at the time it was monumental.

We hired Evan Tierce, a business development person, who proposed that we engage a service to make cold calls. The service could make a hundred calls an hour, and if they connected with the prospect, they would transfer the call to Evan to engage them. Working on his own, Evan could only make twenty calls an hour. The service was going to cost $3,500, which was a significant sum to us at the time. We spent hours debating: Will this work, could this work, is it crazy? Do we get business out of it? We hadn't seen it working in other companies, and cold calling in the CPA industry was unheard of, so there was no precedent for that action.

In the end, we just said, "Let's do it! If we lose the money, so be it." There was the possibility that it could be a better use of Evan's time, so we took the chance to see where his idea would take us. And in the end, he actually turned that $3,500 into $100,000 of new business. Today, we spend $100,000 a year on SalesStaff, a service similar to the one we almost rejected in our early days when we were scared to lose money. We laugh about it today when we remember where we were then and how far we have come since. Thankfully, we were willing to take a chance and fail.

Looking back, we succeeded here because we hired a growth partner who was the right person for the role, and he knew how to develop business. This was consistent with our core belief that every partner should be in the right role, and in particular, that CPAs should be serving clients, not finding new ones. We knew there should be a department dedicated to sales and business development. This fed into our concept of putting the right person in the right role, supporting them, letting them do their job, letting them be the best at what they do, giving them the tools and resources to make them successful, and being willing to let them fail.

This is why we gave Evan the freedom to come up with new ideas and take chances. It was part of our Violent Leadership open door philosophy: there are no bad ideas and no ideas are too crazy, so let's talk about everything.

STRETCHING YOUR CAPACITY FOR RISK

Being willing to fail allowed us to stretch our capacity for risk. Our profession, like many professional service professions, is risk averse.

Setting higher goals can help us stretch our willingness to take risks by forcing us to step beyond our comfort zone. If we want to grow, we have to set goals, and we need to be willing to stretch to reach them. You do not achieve greatness by taking incremental baby steps or maintaining the status quo. You have to step outside the norm. You have to be violent.

Recognizing Risk Aversion

Ask yourself if what you are doing is the same as everyone else. Are you following the crowd, or have you taken an idea and done something completely out of the ordinary? Have you tried something new? What have you done that is different from others in the profession? What separates you from everybody else?

If you have not done any of these things, then what makes you unique, what makes you special? If you are not special, it is likely because you are not willing to step out and be different from the crowd. If you are not getting excellent results, if you are not getting high growth, it is because you are not trying. If you are not reaching your goals, maybe it is because you are not taking the steps and the risks you need to get to them.

Fear of Risk

Often, the first hurdle we run into when we talk about change is fear: fear of the outcome, fear of the unknown, fear of not getting it right. Fear puts the brakes on an organization. It stops progress. But having absolutely no fear can result in recklessness. We need to recognize whether our fear is healthy or destructive.

Stan Raines brings a good balance to our organization. He can share our vision while bringing just enough fear to the table to temper my enthusiasm, to balance it. He does not stop the train, but he applies just enough brake to make me stop and think and review my decision-making process. Have I considered all variables? Stan manages this without overwhelming the company in fear, which is a challenge most companies face when surrounded by four or five fearful partners.

A leader must be empowered to power through others' fear. First, the leader must have the authority to make the decision. If they don't have that authority, they must ask if there are ways to build consensus. Ask yourself:

- Can I sell the idea?

- Do I have what it takes to convince people to follow me and help them see the vision?

- Can I communicate the vision and where it is going?

- Can I paint the picture so they can buy into it enough to follow through once we start?

We once interviewed a very intelligent young man who had a degree in economics rather than accounting. The minute Stan and I met him, we loved him, but we knew that if we brought him in, the other partners would comment on his not being a CPA. We thought they would be against hiring him because he did not fit the traditional mold. We knew the question on everyone's lips would be: Why are we hiring someone with an economics degree when we need a tax person? He would not have gotten an interview at most CPA firms, but we saw something there. He was a good cultural fit for our organization, someone who wanted to be a part of it and grow with us. Stan and I decided to go for it and tell the other partners that they needed to trust our decision. We were going to prove to them that we had made a good choice.

Since the time he joined us, the young man learned the system, learned the people, has been a team player, and has taken ownership of clients. He went back to school to get his hours to become a CPA and worked hard to build his career with us. He has the right skills to be a partner in our firm, and although he is not there yet, if he continues on this path he will get there.

We found that finance people made better analysts, so we started hiring people with finance degrees instead of accounting degrees in some other areas of our firm, rejecting the idea that everybody has to be an accountant to work in an accounting firm. We started hiring based on the potential that someone would be the right fit.

It all started with our willingness to question why we were doing what we were doing. Why did we keep doing things the same way? Is it because that's the way it has always been done? Is there a better way? In this case, we asked: What comes first, the degree or the person? We decided to hire the person first and the degree second—and what we have experienced is almost zero turnover in a profession that has a tremendous retention problem.

Mitigating Fear

Leaders are often fearful of outcomes and their own personal compensation or reward/punishment. Therefore, people want to assure outcomes and avoid risk. It is just like an investment: If you want an assured return, it will be a low-risk investment with a low return. You can open a CD account and get a 1 percent return. It is low, but you can have confidence in it. But if you want a 12 percent return, you will need to take some risk.

The same thing happens in business: people want certainty in the future of their business, and fear makes them resist the decisions that would have a higher reward or allow them to achieve higher goals because those decisions are risky.

You have to remove that barrier. You have to say that it is okay if you take this chance and it does not work. We say to our managers, "Managing your clients and giving them an incredible client experience is your priority. As a result, if you don't meet your billable hours goal, we are not going to penalize you for that. It will not affect your bonus. We want you to take a chance." We remove the fear in them. We ask them to overachieve in one area if we feel that it is better to have them excel at client service than bill an extra hundred hours.

The same goes for our partners. We do not tell them they have to develop $100,000 of business in a year. We tell them to serve the client, and if they do not develop any business, that is okay. Not only do we have other staff members to handle growth, but if a partner serves the client well, they will get referrals. This removes any fear they have of falling short, being fired, or losing compensation. We have learned to manage the process, not the result. Trust the process and the result will come.

The greatest way to mitigate someone's fear is to deal with it and talk about it. First, identify what the fear is and remove the barrier it is creating. Nine times out of ten, barriers are about fear. Once you identify the fear, you can remove the barrier and get a better result from that person.

THE ADVANTAGES OF TAKING RISKS

Trying and failing is what leads to success. When you fail, you learn what not to do—or how to do things better—the next time. This makes you stronger, smarter, and leaner. Good things come out of failure.

Of course, we are talking here about measured risk, not reckless behavior. You can measure risk by setting goals and establishing a strategy to achieve them. You can also set objectives or benchmarks along the way. If you want to grow your business by $50 million over five years, you will need to do some out-of-the-box thinking. If you aim to grow at 20 percent a year, that is going to take some risk. The status quo will not get you to these goals. If your strategy to achieve this growth is to make an acquisition, you can mitigate your risk by conducting a laser-focused targeted search for a specific firm in a specific place with a specific set of criteria that fits you.

Setting goals allows you to retro-engineer your risk. Set your goals, and then start thinking outside the box. If growing at 5 percent a year involves too much risk, dial the goal back to a more manageable level of risk and a commensurate return. Get everyone in a room and ask first: Where do we want to be in five years? Throw a number up there and then break it down to what you need to do to get there. If that path looks too hard or too risky, adjust your goal year on year.

We have noticed that the millennials in our firm are less risk averse than baby boomers. They are far less afraid of failing. They are willing to try things to see if they work, and they do not beat themselves up if they fail. To them, risking failure is preferable to the status quo. They find stagnation boring, so to attract them, you need to be a growing organization with a culture of innovation and energy. You need an organization with Violent Leadership.

RISK AND VIOLENT LEADERSHIP

Without Violent Leadership, you will end up being left behind after the disruption that comes from innovation. We have seen giants fail on this basis. Just as I failed to see the impact of Netflix on the video rental industry, Kodak suffered from the disruption of technological innovation.

That said, recklessness can cause failure, which makes it imperative to find a balance, set goals, and devise a strategy for achieving them. Do not fear pushback within your organization, but do not be stubborn or headstrong; think your ideas through and lead people. You can reflect on objections and decide whether they have validity; if they do, or if somebody raises points you haven't thought of, you should consider them evenhandedly. Assess whether objections have fear in them and, if so, what the level of fear is. This is important—you don't want to ignore the fear's relevance, but you also don't want to let fear be the reason you do not take risks.

This is Violent Leadership in action, creating greatness and success by not fearing failure, by being willing to take a chance and try something different. Reaching out and grabbing what you want is not a passive, risk-free process. It is active. You have to get out there and make it happen. You have to take some chances and lead.

Adopting the Violent Leadership style means that you have to decide what is right and commit to it. Your decisions might not always be popular, and if you make decisions that fail every time, you will not be the leader for very long. This is, again, the backdoor through which fear can creep in, where you find yourself saying, "Oh my goodness, if I keep making bad decisions, I'm not going to . . . " but as a Violent Leader, you have to be able to make the hard decisions and be willing to fail. Importantly, you need to have the confidence in yourself to know that you are making the right decisions. Part of this process is learning whether you are a thermometer or a thermostat—passive or active—in terms of your personality. If you are the former, then finding ways to be active is imperative. We look at this more in the next chapter.

FINAL WORDS

Identify one change in your organization that you are fearful of making but feel passionate about. Identify something you truly believe in and then take that risk. Be the proof of concept. The whole organization does not have to change, only you and your team. Demonstrate success and others will follow. Be willing to change.

Stop penalizing failure. The MLB player that hits .300 is failing 70 percent of the time! Think about that—your team needs more at bats but will only make it if you are not penalizing failure. Keep looking for improvements and areas to change.

CHAPTER 4

ARE YOU A THERMOMETER OR A THERMOSTAT?

THERE ARE GENERALLY TWO types of people in an organization, what I call thermometers and thermostats. The thermostat is someone who sets the temperature, sets the tone. He or she is the regulator and the influencer, the Violent Leader, from whom the energy in the room emanates. As clients walk through our office and as other firm leaders tour the floor, a recurring comment is "Wow, you can feel the energy in this place." What causes that? It starts with the leaders of the firm. We are the energy, and we affect the attitudes of the people we interact with. When we walk around with a positive attitude, stopping by people and asking, "Hey, how's it going?" we are like cheerleaders, we are the buzz, and we are setting a tone that is upbeat and energetic. You can sense the urgency and buzz in our offices, and it is all because, as partners, we are thermostats.

Thermometers, on the other hand, are people who allow the temperature to be set by others or are influenced by others. If I were to walk around with my head down, moping about with a bad attitude, looking as if I am mad at the world and being influenced by the negative environment around me, then I am a thermometer.

We aim to teach our managers to set the tone, not react to outside forces. To have an energetic, positive, and motivated team, managers have to be positive, energetic, and motivational. You don't need a firm full of superstars at every level, but to have an innovative firm, you must have thermostats in key positions setting the temperature.

HOW TO BECOME A THERMOSTAT

I am not a thermostat by nature. It is a learned practice. For some people, it is very natural. They are extroverted. They are up and about. They are talkative. Some people just have that charisma about them. You know them when you meet them, because they are bubbly and positive and they affect people.

I am an introvert. I am happy to stay in my office. It is not natural for me to hang out and shake hands and talk to everyone. I actually have to put "get up and walk around the office" in my calendar. I force myself to do it. I am not faking it—I am sincere, but it has been a learned process for me. I do have innovative energy, but I do not get out and spread it without being disciplined and very pragmatic about it.

We have coached other people on our team in the same way. "Look," we tell them, "you cannot sit in your office with your head down and do your work and pretend that nobody else exists. It is your job to get up and influence others, to encourage, motivate, energize, affect. That is your role, to be a thermostat, and this is how you do it."

It is an ongoing training process for the average introverted CPA to get to the point where he or she exudes interest, positivity, and energy such that people want to be around them because they feel better when they are. This is the evolution of a thermostat—the birth of an influencer.

I realized the importance of being a thermostat in the early days of our firm. I would sit in meetings and hear positive comments about the energy, about how we communicated. I get excited about new ideas, and so I become animated when brainstorming. One day someone told me to bottle my energy and sprinkle it around the room like pixie dust. That was food for thought, so I set about figuring out how to give that to everybody—how do I take what I do and give it to everyone else?

My solution was to just walk about and be around people. If I disciplined myself to interact with them in a way similar to my inter-action in meetings, I figured I would be able to influence them—to pump them up, so to speak, and share my positive energy.

Every day I walk around and stop at each desk for a brief conver-sation. It is usually something personal. I find something positive to say, a word to reinforce the good that I know about that person. I do this on a regular basis, to encourage and motivate them on a personal as well as on a professional level. It is important that people know that we care about their personal lives and their family if we want them to feel like valued members of our family.

The other day, I had a conversation with a manager about his wife and kids and how tough parenting can be in the middle of tax season. I shared some advice from my twenty-six years of marital experience, and we chatted for a little while. One of my partners came to me later and told me that this manager was so appreciative that a partner cared enough about him and his family to spend time talking and helping him out a little bit.

My disciplined actions and regular practice of these learned skills, no matter how uncomfortable it was initially, worked. Just being who I am out in the room with others brought them to the same place.

It is important that this energy is not just emanating from me. I can only do so much, which means it is important that the management team is not sitting in offices with silent heads bowed. They, too, have to get up and interact with and influence people and encourage them to try new things. We are mindful of how we interact with staff members, and they in turn interact with us and other staff members the same way. Stan regularly walks around the office and interacts with people and encourages them. James takes the time to sit down and listen to the team and be an advocate for them and, as a result, inspire them. Part of being a thermostat is inspiring and encouraging others.

When clients walk into our office, they comment on the sense of excitement, the urgency, and the energy of the room. They ask, "Hey, how do you get this out of your team?" The answer is that my partners and I just do it—we set the tone, we set the temperature, and we generate the energy in the room. Then most people in the room react to us and the energy carries throughout the firm. Each partner is taking action, whether it is outside their comfort zone or not, and effectively disrupts the status quo. In this way, each partner and each person that partner talks to is embracing Violent Leadership.

Admittedly, if people were not being treated well by an organization and its leadership, they might not care how excited their manager was, but our firm's transparency, our willingness to try new ideas, and the value we place on each team member makes the thermostat-styled leadership the final ingredient in our innovative corporate culture.

MAXIMIZE YOUR THERMOSTATIC EFFECT

The way to maximize your thermostatic effect is to increase your interactions with the team. Aside from walking around the offices, we have an open door policy, include people in meetings, and teach and train the people to have the same approach. This not only maximizes the leadership's reach, it perpetuates the culture companywide.

These professional interactions are not the only way to maximize the buzz and energy. In our three offices, we have added shuffle-board, a putting green, a ping-pong table, a pool table, a Golden Tee machine, a chess board, and a cornhole toss. These fun interactions create positive energy and excitement. We found that it is okay to have a little fun at the office, and it maximizes the effect you can have on the "temperature" of the team.

SOLUTIONS-FOCUSED LEADERSHIP

Part of being a thermostat and fostering a proactive culture within your firm involves fostering a solutions-based ethic. We tell our clients, "Ideas, answers, results—it is what we do." Then we work to set that tone, that temperature in our office. This means that if you walk into our office with a complaint, we welcome your feedback, but only if you are able to propose a solution along with it. If you want to complain without searching for a solution, we do not want to hear it. We do not have a complaint department—we have a solutions department, which is a culture that is focused on ideas, answers, and results. You have a problem or maybe you don't know exactly what the problem is. Tell me what the symptoms are and let's talk about what you are seeing, hearing, and feeling. Let's get to the root of the problem and look for creative ideas to improve and make the situation better. What do you suggest we do to make it better?

Complaints are opportunities to support the solutions culture. Technical or other questions often arise, and if team members feel they can just come to me for the solutions, that is not teaching them to be solution focused and problem solvers.

Therefore, by introducing a solutions department we changed the entire dynamic of our office. There will always be opportunities to complain and to seek answers to the many questions and problems encountered in the office. By creating a solutions-focused atmosphere, we have created a proactive culture that prohibits whining and pushes a complainer to find a solution, or pushes them out altogether. This aspect of Violent Leadership lends itself to those who truly look for answers and encourages them to seek out the solutions to problems.

A tax manager came to me with a problem that I believed she should have been able to solve herself. We were looking at a complex tax matter, and while I knew the solution, I also knew that if I did not encourage her to seek it out, she would never learn. "Lupita, you should know the answer to this. You need to find the solution," I said, and pointed her to the research. "The answer is in this book. You need to figure this out on your own, because me just giving you the answer is not what we're about."

For her to focus on solutions, I had to push back and say, "Don't just bring me the problem or question without at least attempting to find a solution. It made her angry at the time, but during her review about a year later, she thanked me.

"I didn't realize at the time what I was doing," she said, "but what it made me do, it built my confidence and made me realize I'm better at this than I thought. I do know how to find answers and solutions. I do have the resources. I just needed to know that I should be looking for them."

The result later played itself out in a complex oil and gas tax situation. Lupita brought me a situation and this time offered a solution. When I asked her about her process, she said, "I just took the Oil & Gas Guide home and read it until I found the answer." The Violent Leadership culture was working; we had become a solutions-based firm.

GETTING OUT OF THE THERMOMETER ZONE

Many leaders who are thermometers allow the people around them to set the temperature when they need to be the one doing it. People might be comfortable at seventy degrees, but as a leader you have to be able to say, "This will work better at sixty-eight, so that is where we are going." This is where the philosophy of Violent Leadership comes into play. It is like a blast of cold air in a hot and stuffy room, affecting and disrupting the "temperature" of others in the room. It demands that you actively set the level of energy, excitement, and urgency.

If you are a thermometer by nature, it is important to put some processes in place to become a thermostat. Ask yourself, "What am I doing?" "Am I influencing my company?" "What can I do to exert greater influence?"

Are you a thermostat naturally? If so, own that role and act on it. Take control of the atmosphere around you and change it. Be that Violent Leader. Control your surroundings and take steps to turn the heat up or down. Measure the temperature and decide what is needed to change the environment around you.

The next step is to examine your actions, emotions, and demeanor. Your demeanor influences people around you, so it is important to look at how you are presenting yourself and what tone, mood, and energy you are portraying as you interact with those around the office. In this ever more virtual world that we live in of emails, texts, and chats, your expressions are even more important, as there is no facial expression or body language by which to communicate with. If it is not consistent with being a thermostat, then you need to get proactive about changing that. You need to be setting the energy level, setting the tone, setting the enthusiasm. Start with simply being nice, then add a little interest in others, then pour some energy into encouraging and motivating them. Take an interest in their family life or their personal interests. Tell them they are doing a great job, or if you see an opportunity for constructive coaching, take a moment and do that. Express an appreciation for their sense of urgency or, on the back of the compliment, suggest they adopt a sense of urgency to gain extra energy for their tasks. It is important to be sincere in this. Trust is lost with insincerity; you truly have to care.

In our firm, we involve all our managers in interpersonal leadership skills training, including how to influence others. That training comes from outside the organization. I highly recommend that you ensure that your managers are equipped with these skills so that they can take on the Violent Leadership role.

If you are an introvert who would happily go all day without talking to anyone, set a time in your schedule where you say, "Okay, it is time to get up and go do this."

It is like Fitbit. I wear one on my wrist, and every hour it notifies me that I have to get up and take 250 steps. It is my reminder that it is time to get up and walk around the office and make sure I'm encouraging people. It does not have to be everybody at the same time, but reaching out and interacting with people allows them to feel and absorb positive energy.

For me, Violent Leadership is about not accepting that I am an introverted accountant. Sitting in my office with my head down is *not* okay. Here the Violent Leader says, "No, check yourself, get up, do what you know is necessary to be that type of leader." Do not resign yourself to "This is who I am." That is not a good excuse. It's average. It's mediocre. You have to be more than that. If you are going to be great, you have to push yourself to be better than you are.

FINAL WORDS

Examine your attitude and actions every day. Ask yourself how you are influencing your own company. If you are not moving the company positively forward, look for ways to innovate on your own.

Recognize that you set the tone, that your energy starts the momentum that carries through the firm, establishes the culture, and affects the way people respond to you. If you are a quiet, negative person, that is the tone you are setting for your organization, whether you realize it or not. If you want a certain kind of organization, set that tone, be the thermostat, be that person. It may be hard to do, but you need to know that you can, and must, do it.

CHAPTER 5

CHOOSING YOUR HAT
THE VIOLENT WAY

"WE SHOULD GET UP every morning, look for new business, service our clients, and manage our practice." Did that sentence wear you out? The days of being all things to all people are long gone in firms that are positioning themselves for intentional growth and success. One partner may be a rainmaker but that same partner is probably not the best at serving the client and delivering a quality client experience. One person cannot do this alone. Each person will bring a unique and valuable skill set to the team and we should focus on that talent. In the traditional professional services model, CPAs or other service providers are expected to spend their time developing new business, serving their clients, and excelling in their professional role. They are spread so thin across their different roles that they do not develop expertise in any of them. Firms that continue this practice will be challenged to grow and progress.

In the traditional professional services model, CPAs or other service providers are expected to spend their time developing new business, serving their clients, *and* excelling in their professional role. They are spread so thin across their different roles that they do not develop expertise in any of them.

In this old model, CPAs grind out the work when it is busy and put the sales effort to the side. Then when it comes time to deliver a memorable experience to the client or to mentor and develop the team, they cannot do it, because they are worried about developing new business and getting the work out the door. We do not have the time to give each area the attention it deserves.

It is time for a new model: the Violent Leadership model. These days, to be an effective leader you need to think like a Violent Leader. You need to be willing to take the risk and shake up the organization to ensure that everyone is doing the job that they were put on this earth to do—including you. You cannot wear every hat and be effective, so it is important to identify the positions you need to fill, shift your people into those roles according to their strengths, and find better people to fill the other seats.

There are essentially three different areas in a business. The first is production, which is what your business does. If you are in the air conditioning business, you have people who install air conditioning units and repair them. Next is sales and marketing, and finally, the administration of the firm, including recruiting and retention and the financial side. As a leader, you need to know which of these hats you should be wearing and which people can wear the other hats better. I am a longtime CPA and serve my clients well, but as an executive, there is always a risk of getting bogged down in the firm's administration. I can be the administrator or I can be the strategist who leads the organization and places people around me to do the rest. I can do one of these jobs, but I cannot do them all. This means I need to let other people wear certain hats, not get in my own way, and do what I am best at.

There was a time when I did the financials myself and spent more time digging into the details of the firm and producing financial statements than I did being a CPA. I was analyzing metrics and compiling financial statements to share with other partners. It was a necessary part of our firm, but it consumed half of my time. As a result, my clients became secondary and my customer service began to slip. I was not returning phone calls or emails promptly. Managers would bring me returns to sign, but I was so busy that I set them aside and held up the process. Not only was I failing in the client service area, but I found I had no time or energy for strategy and innovation—one of my most important roles.

I was putting in twice the hours but being half as effective, because I was doing something that was not my strength. It was not the best use of my skills and time. I was doing it because it needed to be done—not because I was passionate about doing it. My best skill is planning and advising clients, but once I put on the CFO hat, everything suffered.

After many late nights at the office, I realized I needed to change the way we did things. I needed to get Violent, step out of my comfort zone, take a financial risk, and hire someone to fill the financial/ administrative role. Not only was I able to increase my revenue production in an amount equal to the salary of this new role, but my late nights became earlier, the analysis and reporting became consistent, reliable, and effective, I endured less stress, and the management team was happy to have current, accurate data by which to make decisions. Ultimately, I could focus on doing what I do best. The benefit of letting someone else wear that hat is measurable.

It is important to avoid getting bogged down. Work needs to be done, but if you are not a CFO by nature, you can easily start drowning in administrative work or back office work instead of growing and developing your company.

The bottom line is that your company cannot grow if you are not out leading it. Your leadership and high-level performance is what is going to make the firm successful—let someone else deal with the other tasks.

THE VIOLENT LEADER'S HAT

When you choose to wear the hat of the Violent Leader, you may find your old leadership style left a bit of a mess. To streamline your transition into a more proactive, focused, and innovative style, you need to sit down and map out what the needs of your organization are. At first, you may not have the resources to transform everything that needs transforming, but ranking your needs in order of importance, recognizing what has the most impact, and prioritizing what you should not be doing frees you up to do what you are best at. Your organization may not have the resources just yet to allow you to wear just one hat. In that case, it is important that you recognize and identify the various hats you wear, to avoid getting bogged down.

Look at where you are spending the most time and decide if that is helping the business or the organization grow or be better. Do not get bogged down in details. Delegate to people with the right demeanor and skill set—they will do the job better than you.

As a Violent Leader, your job is to identify how you can grow the firm, how you can move the firm forward, and how you can bring people in to compensate for your areas of weakness. Again, there is strength in recognizing your weaknesses. Having the courage to change does not only apply to your organization, it applies to you as well, and being willing to own and compensate for your weaknesses by surrounding yourself with people who can do a particular task better is the mark of an effective Violent Leader.

WORKING ON THE COMPANY

Leaders need to work *on* the company instead of working for the company or the organization.

In our firm, Stan is in charge of HR. He is a strong leader. He is particularly good at setting the right tone for the department—he is definitely a thermostat who radiates positive energy. However, if you were to ask him to monitor employee vacation days or ensure that everybody's bios are up to date on the company website, he would lose his laser focus. While it is part of HR, if he were to do all that he would get bogged down, and that would take away from his primary goal: working *on* the organization.

Everyone at a partner level needs to identify their strengths, the tasks they are good at. For example, I am not going to take a great CPA who has weak interpersonal skills and send him off to sales training. It would be better to play to his strength. It is better to have him wear the CPA hat and build around that.

Let us say a partner has 1,500 billable hours as opposed to the 1,100 that we asked for; that tells me he is working for the company and not working on the company. He is taking the extra 400 hours a year and sitting down and working for the company like a good technician cranking out work. He is not developing people or nurturing clients to grow the practice. He is not doing what we need as an organization to grow and get better.

There is nothing wrong with what he is doing, necessarily, but the more of a leader you are, the more you need to work on the company by developing others and leading the way. You need to wear the hat that makes everybody around you better. This is an essential component of Violent Leadership.

REMOVING THE BUSINESS DEVELOPMENT HAT

One of the first revolutionary decisions we made in our firm was to take the sales expectations and quotas away from CPAs. To understand how unusual this is, you have to first understand that, in our profession, one of the top concerns is growth. There are organizations that exist specifically to teach CPAs how to sell and be rainmakers. Generally speaking, CPAs are not salespeople. In a profession that has made sales training and growth a priority, we decided not to expect this from our CPAs. This went against the advice of the experts—in one meeting, the managing partner of a top 100 CPA firm told me, matter-of-factly, that our process would fail.

Our philosophy was to make better use of the CPAs' time and focus on their strengths, not their weaknesses. We said, "Hey, you know what? We are not going to force you to be salespeople. We want you to wear the hat you went to school for and you're best at, which is advising clients." Then we hired a salesperson and created a team within our organization that generates leads, follows up with the prospects, and develops new business, which the CPA then closes.

The result has been the addition of two more sales professionals, annual growth in excess of 25 percent per year, and happier partners in the firm. We had a senior tax manager join our firm specifically because we eliminated his $100,000 per year sales quota. He was so uncomfortable wearing that hat, he chose our firm. He said the number-one reason he moved over was being told he did not have a sales quota. "So I will not have this hanging over my head that if I do not develop $100,000, I may get fired?" he asked. "No, I do not want you to develop anything," I said. "Don't worry about it. I do not need you to be a good salesman. I need you to be a CPA." He flourished at our firm without that additional pressure, and within the first ninety days he got $40,000 in referrals. The bottom line is that if a CPA just does a great job and is happy, they will get referrals. They do not need to try to be a salesperson.

Most firms have a very convoluted way of growing the practice that places individuals in positions they are not really cut out for. In practice, when a CPA is referred a new client, it is that CPA who keeps the client and performs the service, no matter their expertise or the needs of the client. Why? Because a CPA's compensation is generally impacted by the amount of revenue they manage. In most firms, it can be financially punitive to let go of a referral. But we believed that simply because a CPA is referred to a client does not mean that CPA is the best one to serve that client. He or she could be wearing the wrong hat.

For us, wearing the right hat involved going out and hiring a sales leader, Evan, who was not a CPA. We tasked Evan with growing the firm and then allowed him to do his job. It was not long before Evan began to demonstrate what Violent Leadership looked like. He put the sales tools he needed in front of us, starting with account-ability for the sales process.

Step by step, Evan pushed us out of our comfort zone. We imple-mented Salesforce and inbound marketing. We implemented a cold calling regimen to develop leads, and when we got referrals we gave them to Evan to follow up and develop, because we believed that CPAs are just not good at following up on sales leads and nurturing new prospects. In our process, if a CPA gets a referral, it must be turned over to our sales team to nurture, develop, and onboard. That way, we know it will be placed with the right person and followed up on correctly, rather than left with a CPA who is not the best person for that work.

Our practice growth team is incredible at nurturing leads, and as a result, our close rate and success rate went through the roof. Our clients are better served by matching the needs of the client with the expert in that area.

Challenging that status quo disrupted the CPA's compensation, and that was a scary path to take. The innovation inherent in Violent Leadership allowed us to take a process that was universally managed differently in our profession and turn it over to someone who had that expertise. Implementing this process involved taking the administrative role away from CPAs and saying, "Don't worry about this. You need to worry about serving the clients. You will get referrals because you are doing a great job, but when that happens, pass that referral to Evan and let him take it from there."

We challenged the status quo, disrupted an accepted practice, and took the risk that this was best for our clients. Essentially, we created a one-firm culture. Ours is not a firm of multiple partners working individually under one banner. Our clients are clients of the firm, not the partner who was referred.

Executing the Violent Leadership style demanded that we take chances and risks that could have had a personal economic cost. The result, however, was very positive.

REMOVING THE CLIENT SERVICE HAT

Another area that CPAs traditionally are not great at is client service, even if we think that we are. We think returning a phone call is great client service. But by Apple standards or Four Seasons standards, that is not the case. Great client service happens at a much higher level than just returning a phone call; at that level, it becomes an experience.

To avoid CPAs dropping the ball, we took what was previously an administrative assistant/tax processing role and repurposed it into a client service role. Some of the tasks remain the same, but now the role is focused on taking the client experience to the next level. We took that hat away from our CPAs and said, "Here's what we are going to do. We are going to make sure we have a team in place so that nothing falls through the cracks from a communication perspective."

Leaders have many hats to choose from and need to be careful in choosing them. But putting the right people in the right hats is not just an issue for leadership. In the next chapter, we look at how you can filter this leadership style beyond your management team and into the company at large.

FINAL WORDS

To be an effective Violent Leader, you may need to restructure the organization so that everyone is doing the job they're meant to do. This includes you; you cannot wear every hat and be effective. Focus on your strengths and delegate your weak tasks to those who can excel.

Your job is to grow the business, to work *on* the company rather than for the company. Recognize the weaknesses in your own business and surround yourself with people who fill in those gaps. These are signs of a successful Violent Leader.

CHAPTER 6

IT TAKES A VILLAGE
TO RUN A FIRM

DAVID MAISTER'S BOOK *Managing a Professional Services Firm* is a professional services classic describing three roles necessary for a successful consulting practice—finders, minders, and grinders.[8] These roles form the common professional service village. It is a commonly accepted practice that all three of these roles—those who find the client, those who mind the client, and those who grind away at the work—are all found in a successful professional organization. It is akin to the hunter mentality, in that somebody has to go out and hunt food, somebody has to clean it and prepare it for consumption, and somebody has to keep the house clean or the house straight.

---

8   David Maister, *Managing a Professional Services Firm* (New York: Free Press, 1993).

In the last chapter, we looked at how the partners and owners need to delineate their roles according to strengths rather than try to fill these roles in the traditional way. There is a common misperception in most professional service firms, specifically CPA firms, that these roles belong to the partners or owners. As owners, the finder was the hunter, the one who brought in the new clients. That person has always had the most power in the firm, because they generated the business that started the firm and then kept the firm going. Nevertheless, you cannot exist without the other roles—someone (the minder) has to take care of the business, and someone (the grinder) has to do the actual work. As Maister explains, specific roles are needed in an organization to make it successful.

The philosophy of putting the right people in the right roles extends beyond the partner level and into the company as a whole. A successful organization needs the right person in a sales role, client service role, and revenue generation role. It needs people doing the actual work.

This is where Violent Leadership comes into play. Today, the roles played by the owners and partners as finders, minders, and grinders have been disrupted by technology. Professional service organizations need strong client experience and client service departments, strong practice or business growth departments, and strong revenue-producing components, which is precisely why the owners shouldn't try to play all roles and should just stick to their own hat. This evolution of the roles and skills and the technology disruption in the profession has spawned a new village, a village that changes the roles from finders, minders, and grinders to servers, solvers, and advisors. This chapter looks at these new roles in depth, as Violent Leadership proactively updates the outmoded professional services business model to the more relevant new village model today.

Just before we left MillerBrown, Jon Meadows, a close and trusted tax manager, left us and went to work for another CPA firm. Jon is both an attorney and a CPA, and a very intelligent, technically competent, and personable individual. Several months after we left MillerBrown and launched MRZ, Stan reached out to Jon and asked him to come in and talk about why he left. As we began to talk about his current role in the firm he'd joined, Jon expressed how uncomfortable he was with the new firm's expectations for him. It was forcing him to make PowerPoint presentations to various trade organizations and gave him a large sales quota that he felt he could not meet.

"Look, you don't have to be a salesman here," I told him. "You don't have to get up in front of a crowd and give presentations. In fact, you will never have to make a public speech again. We will play to your strengths so that you can do what you do best. We will put you in our village and you will play your role."

Jon was visibly relieved, and ultimately he agreed to join us as a partner. The result is that over the last four years Jon has had a tremendous amount of success. He has gone from managing $400,000 or $500,000 to well over $1.6 million, and he has yet to make a public speech. Not only that, he has generated more business than the quota he was originally given at his previous firm. He tripled the business he brought in, because he was given a role that plays to his strengths and had the support of other players in our organization, such as the sales team and client relationship manager.

This is a perfect example of why we have a new village with a division of labor that plays to each villager's strength.

THE MILLENIALS

Have you noticed? The millenials are here. They've arrived in full force and are impacting organizations. They have been educated differently than we were, and their focus is more on what they do best. They are also more focused on balance in their lives. All of this is forcing professional services firms to have a laser focus when assigning them roles in our firms. It requires a deep dive into specialization.

This millennial generation is not concerned with selling new business. Students today are developing more specialized skills. They didn't get an education to be a salesperson; they want to have purpose in their career and in their life. They want to be taught how to be leaders, how to be exceptional at their job, how to be really great in their role. They certainly do not want to be forced into something they do not want or something they are not good at. They do not want to be forced into sales if they are not naturally salespeople. Forcing people to do something that is outside their core competency does not create a sustainable company.

If you want to grow your company, be that Violent Leader and adopt the new village strategy. Stop trying to force people into roles that don't fit them; instead, play to their strengths and support the development of their leadership and technical skills. Have people with the right talent focus on sales and practice growth and development inside the organization, and allow the CPA to focus on what they do best. The firm grows as a result.

DISRUPTIVE TECHNOLOGY

As early as 2013, Oxford University reported that there is a 94 percent probability of the computerization of accounting and auditing occupations within the next twenty years.[9] It is clear from this report and others that two of the jobs most susceptible to technology disruption are tax preparers and auditors. If we are to survive, we must get ahead of the technology disruption wave and position ourselves as advisors. You need to take a hard look at your firm and be ready to adopt a new structure. This requires a shift from compliance-based roles to roles focusing on solutions, providing answers, solving problems, and anticipating the future for clients—and advising them on their companies as opposed to taking historical information and giving them a product in return. We need to transform from a profession that focuses on historical data into one that looks to the future and anticipates change for our clients and advises them on that path forward.

Technology is disrupting the professional service professions, replacing data entry and the grind of the work in general. Those who fail to adopt the new village roles of servers, solvers, and advisors will eventually find that the grinders in the village will no longer have a valuable or meaningful role.

Violent Leadership is needed to disrupt the current technological disruption. We must abandon the past and embrace and empower the new village.

A NEW VILLAGE OF SERVERS, SOLVERS, AND ADVISORS

Having an effective village is about having a culture in place that plays to the strength of the owners and revenue producers and supports them with a team of experts that serve the client and grow and serve

---

9   Carl B. Frey and Michael Osborne, "The Future of Employment: How Susceptible Are Jobs to Computerisation?" (Oxford Martin Programme on Technology and Employment, Working Paper, 2013).

the firm. It is about having a culture that does not force roles onto people that they should not be doing. When people are aligned with what they do best, we reinforce their strengths, minimize our weakness, and end up with a better organization and better culture. People are happier. It is not that they are not challenged, it is just that they are not being forced into areas that are outside their core competencies.

It is time to focus on having an organization where our people are problem solvers and advisors with a client-centric approach that creates a memorable experience for our clients and fulfills the business needs of the firm. This requires a paradigm shift from the way we currently think as service professionals.

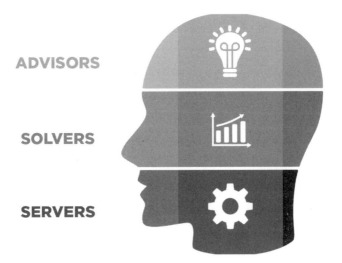

Servers

- Client experience officer
  - Oversees client relationship managers
- Client relationship manager
  - Serves clients

- Delivers the actual "deliverable" product to the client

- Is the funnel for all client interaction

- Chief administrative officer

  - Manages all aspects of the firm: technology, CRM, finance, facilities

  - Reports to managing partner

- Chief financial officer

  - Analyzes performance data and prepares reports for CPAs

- Brand experience officer

  - Marketing

  - Brand management

  - Internal marketing

  - Culture marketing

- Practice growth partner

  - Manages brand experience officer

  - Identifies prospects, problems, or issues they may have

  - Connects to the right partner

  - This is the business development role

- Employee experience officer

  - Serves the people in our organization

  - Teaches the culture

  - Recruits new talent

Solvers

- These are the revenue producers of the firm, from staff level through manager.

- They deal in historical information.

- We are developing them to be focused on solving client problems.

- In our tagline, *Ideas. Answers. Results*, they are driving the answers and results.

Advisors

- Primarily our partners; although no one is excluded from this, our partners *must* be advisors and solvers.

- Staff members transition from solvers to advisors over time.

- These are the "Ideas" in our tagline. We do solve problems, so solver still applies to the group.

- They take historical data and advise clients on the future and anticipate changes and the future.

SERVERS

Servers are the more traditional operational and support services inside an organization. Traditionally, they have focused inwardly, not outwardly on how the client experiences the firm.

Two years ago, I proposed to my partners that the role of the executive assistants, tax return processors, report processors, and similar roles needed to be repurposed. Rather than focus on a process within the firm, these roles needed to focus on the needs and experience of the client. As part of our Violent Leadership philosophy, we took these traditional roles and redefined them in the new village. Our servers are client relationship managers (CRM), chief administrative officer (CAO), practice growth partners, and employee experience officers (EEO).

This repurposing may seem obvious, but it has been revolutionary within the professional services industry and can be attributed entirely to the proactive desire to be a catalyst for change by leveraging Violent Leadership philosophy.

Client Experience Officer

We introduced a client experience officer position to focus on how our clients experience working with us. This revolutionary role is a leadership role whose purpose is to measure, enhance, develop, and make memorable the client experience.

Kevynn Brewer, our Client Experience Officer, takes client experience to a new level. She leads the CRM team, trains and teaches them, and develops new ways of working to make our client experience better.

Her first effort to measure our client experience was with the implementation of the Net Promoter Score, a one-question survey that is commonly used by many Fortune 500 companies known for their client experience, such as Disney, Apple and American Express. We ask, "On a scale of 0 to 10, with 10 being highest, what is the likelihood that you would recommend us (our company) to a friend or colleague?" It is the measure of how satisfied a customer is and whether they would refer us to somebody else. It's a key question, because if a customer refers us to someone else, they are a promoter of our business. If someone's response is not positive, our client experience officer follows up with that client and works to turn it into a positive situation to make sure that client is 100 percent satisfied. She looks at their entire experience with our firm—how the return was delivered, how easy it was, how easy it was to get information, whether we communicated effectively, and whether we responded on time.

Strong interpersonal skills make for a great client experience officer. Our officer is a happy person with a thermostat set to positive, empathetic, and reassuring. If you are mad and you talk to her, your mood will shift. CPAs as a rule do not have that sort of outgoing personality, which is why our officer is better suited to that hat. Her job is to make people happy, and she enjoys doing that.

Client Relationship Managers

We started restructuring our village by taking the grinder administrative work and turning it into a server or client relationship role.

Our CRMs were put in place to create a memorable client experience. Creating this role meant being willing to adopt a new process in our service to clients. Service had to evolve beyond "You give me information. I put it on the return. I give it back to you." Everybody does that. We needed our clients to have an experience that sets us apart from every other organization. To accomplish that, we shifted the focus of our executive assistants and tax processors away from internal processes and toward the client. People who were historically administrative executive assistants, focused on serving the needs of the owner, were repurposed to focus on making the client's experience better. Instead of being the executive assistant to the partner, they became the internal voice and advocate for our client.

Our CRMs are empowered to serve the client and solve client service problems. They are better at the interaction because they have the right personality for handling client service relationships, and they are trained in interpersonal skills.

From the moment a new client comes through the door, they are handed off to their CRM, who manages all interactions for the team. The CRM makes sure the information that comes in goes to the right place. They make sure work gets out the door. Each client therefore knows that for anything they need, they have one person to go to. They know the CRM will not solve all their problems but will know who can. The client relationship manager will make sure their needs are met, whatever they are.

We started with one person in this role, Blanca Pena, our lead CRM, and now have a client relationship team of six people. Their only job is to manage the client experience and make it a great one.

Chief Administrative Officer

Do you have an office manager or firm administrator who really does more than just that role? A server in our new village, we redefined this role to be one that makes the firm the only client. Our CAO's role is to serve the firm as her client and manage the administration of the firm. Emily Mazey is our CAO and she is responsible for making sure everything gets done. The administration of the entire firm runs through her, so while she may not do the financials, she makes sure the financials are done on time. She makes sure the payroll is done, and the bills are paid, and the facilities are managed.

She makes sure that what the executive committee puts in place is executed. Essentially, if something needs to happen, she is the person to make it so. I don't have to worry about whether the light bill was paid, whether someone got a paycheck, whether we have water and coffee, whether all our licenses are in place and our own tax return filed. Our CAO does that. She makes life easier for everyone by serving the firm.

Chief Financial Officer

Do you have a CFO or a controller in your organization? Most professional service firms do, and usually accountants fill these roles. However, as a Violent Leader, I was compelled to take a closer look at the role and its responsibilities. What I discovered was that the CFO role was better served by an analyst, not a CPA.

The CFO needs to analyze financial data and give it to the partners so that they can better manage their individual practice areas, and thus ultimately better manage the firm. Analyzing data is difficult and time consuming for CPAs. We needed someone who could do this and give meaningful feedback so that the partners didn't have to run their own reports and try to figure out "Where are we? Where am I? How am I doing?" on their own.

Therefore, we made a radical shift, from hiring an accountant as the CFO or controller to hiring someone with a completely different skill set. Our CFO has a degree in finance, not in accounting, because we needed someone with more analytical skills serving the management team with relevant and actionable data. Providing data such as realization and utilization may have value, but what does the service team need to do with the data? What does it mean? These items are just one small piece to the firm and are not the end all be all for decisions. We look at capacity and how the team is performing as a whole, including NPS metrics and average delivery time of services, and production data that projects where the team will be and where the delivery bottlenecks are. By listening to our partners, we started giving them data with two or three solutions for improvement. We find these metrics only point to a more in depth opportunity for improvement.

How much time does your partner and manager team spend mining data or reports? When we asked our partners how we could help them be more efficient, this was one of the issues we uncovered. They were spending time looking at data and running reports that they didn't find useful, and they simply didn't know what to do with the data. Partners and managers are here to serve clients and they can focus more of their effort on that. They no longer have to try to figure out their team's billable hours, or how the team is performing, or what the team's metrics are. The financial analyst gives them that data on a monthly basis and says, "This is how you are doing. Here are the areas that are below and above average. Here are the things that are slacking. Here are the things that are working great." Instead of having to spend an hour or two a week on extracting that data and trying to analyze it, the CPA can now just see the data and use it to better manage their practice.

Redefining the CFO role made the CPAs more aware of what was going on with their team. It made them more efficient and more profitable because they could see more quickly what was working and what was not. No longer do we go a whole tax season before we figure out that someone on the team isn't meeting their budgeted hours.

Once the CFO took the job of analysis off the CPAs, the CPAs were free to serve our clients properly.

Practice Growth Partner

The traditional professional service firm will typically take a revenue-generating partner who has demonstrated an above average skill in developing new business and make them the partner in charge of growing the firm. We broke the mold here. Instead of hiring a CPA to take on the role of a practice growth partner, we hired Evan Tierce who was great at developing relationships, had some business acumen, had sales experience, and knew what a sales organization would look like inside a firm. Because he was not a CPA, as that role traditionally is, this hire was definitely outside the box.

We gave Evan the responsibility to grow the firm. Developing new business was his number-one goal. When someone gets a referral, we turn it over to him. He then makes the calls, sets up appointments, nurtures the prospect, gathers data, and makes sure we have the right person assigned to do the work for this potential client. By the time we get to the meeting, we can actually have a real conversation based on the research our practice growth partner has developed.

In essence, this partner finds ways to develop new leads and turn them into clients. He also manages the marketing department, since that is an area of growth that generates leads for our firm. This includes our website and blog and anything that develops business at our firm.

Employee Experience Officer

We redefined the role of the human resource manager to be an EEO. Although the role involves traditional HR management responsibilities, we see it as so much more than just HR. As a server, Amanda Shook is not a manager, although there are tasks to be managed. She looks at how our people experience MRZ: What do they do? How do they interact? How can we improve our employees' experience and serve them better?

Our EEO handles all the onboarding of new employees, making sure all the benefits are in place, developing new benefits, and creating ideas for benefits. She does all the interviewing and recruiting. She does the culture training, so when someone joins our firm, it is her job to make that a great experience. When somebody leaves the firm, she handles that as well. She instituted unlimited paid time off and orchestrated a "mother's room" for the nursing mothers in the firm.

To serve in this role, a person must be able to be both a servant leader and an employee advocate. It is a tough role. It is also important that people feel they can trust her. The thermostat setting for this role is energetic, bright, and with the empathy and interpersonal skills to handle the nuances of normal human relationships.

Brand Experience Officer

Our brand experience officer is not just a marketing director. Catherine Seitz handles all the external relations and communications of the firm, including marketing.

We repurposed and redefined this role because it is responsible for more than just marketing. Internally, our brand experience officer handles our communication from blogs to newsletters. Externally, she handles public relations.

It is her job to market the firm and market our brand from the outside inasmuch as how the public experiences our brand. Her work is often the front line in how we are perceived and makes our first impression on potential clients.

SOLVERS AND ADVISORS

Partners as Solvers and Advisors

Too many firms are still in that compliance, delivery of a tax return, and delivery of an audit mentality, which they believe is all they do.

However, these functions are being replaced by technology at a very fast pace. As a result, we need to shift from a preparer to a solver and advisor mentality.

The solvers in our company are at the staff level up through manager. As they come up through the organization, they focus on solving problems. We are developing everyone in our firm to be advisors. While today this level is found at the partner and manager level, we are proactively changing our learning process to be one that has everyone on the path to being an advisor.

Our partners do not just produce tax returns or audits or financial statements. Our profession is being disrupted with cloud technology and artificial intelligence (AI) that will replace the data entry performed by many of the staff. To adapt to the current technological disruption, we are moving partners from compliance to consulting and have them focus on solving whatever problem a client has. They are taught in our organization, in our culture, that we are here to anticipate clients' problems and solve them.

Our partners and CPAs are moving from being compliance oriented—that is, looking in the rearview mirror—to being problem solvers. Much of what we do is solving problems, advising clients on future situations, and consulting with them on decisions they need to make. True to Violent Leadership philosophy, this approach is forward looking and proactive rather than reactive.

The CPAs focus just on their role—revenue generation in their specific niche and industry specialty. Each partner has a niche and a certain amount of business he or she manages. We ask our CPAs to develop something at which they are experts, and that becomes their primary focus. Mine is oil and gas and real estate. Those are two areas that I love, and my focus is growing those areas and being an expert in them.

When we develop a deep dive into specialty areas and with a high level of expertise, this allows our salespeople to go out and say, "We have an expert in oil and gas. We have an expert in the medical field." The CPAs themselves do not have to be rainmakers, but they have a responsibility to see their area grow—they have to participate in the growth of the practice. They do not have to knock on doors, they do not have the pressure of needing ten new leads every day, but they need to engage with our practice growth departments. They can do this by writing blogs, or teaching a CPE at a law firm, or doing some public speaking that shows them as an expert in their area. Our sales and marketing team then take that and market it.

Our CPAs do not have to attend social, trade association, or other industry events. We have our own networking events, called "meet ups," where we invite a select few with whom we want to network, as opposed to going to some association meeting that does not have the right people to interact with, such as decision makers. Networking is important, but we have not found that making everybody in the firm do some networking every month is effective. We've seen other firms mandate this level of networking, but we just ask, "Why? Show us the results of that." It sounds like a good practice, but when you measure it, do you get meaningful results? It is like a shotgun approach. We prefer our more targeted meet ups, ones that include decision makers and serve a particular purpose.

Associates and Managers as Solvers

Ideas. Answers. Results. It is our value proposition, and this is indoctrinated into our team. At the staff level, we teach and train problem solving. As the staff person progresses from a solver, they learn to be advisors. We are adding training for staff at all levels to develop these skills, which we believe are imperative to our long-term success.

Practice Growth as Solvers

Our practice growth team members are also solvers in our village. They focus on identifying what problems or issues a prospect is having and then offering our advisors and solvers as a solution. Our business development's focus is solving problems, not for our clients but for those who are not yet clients. We have had tremendous success by focusing on what issues a prospect is having and offering ourselves as a solution. This has helped grow our firm.

Brand Experience as Solvers

Another reason the old model of finders, minders, and grinders falls short in our current climate is that it does not describe the practice growth and marketing once you remove the revenue generators—the partners, owners, and CPAs—from the finder category.

Today, we have to look at the whole brand experience—marketing, social media, and content curation—as part of the solver's role. Our tools and our approach are different from most companies. As mentioned briefly earlier, we use inbound marketing strategies. Inbound marketing is a technique for drawing customers to products and services via content marketing, social media marketing, and search engine optimization. We develop content internally and publish it to drive people to our firm. We are focused on writing and authority marketing.

Our brand experience officer and our marketing and business development departments are focused on prospective clients, but they are all focused on solving their problems. Our marketing team focuses on how the client perceives and experiences our brand, making sure that the content we are putting out focuses on solving problems for our clients and our prospects. It makes sure that our branding impresses the client with a preview of the experience they can expect to have with us.

FINAL WORDS

Take a Violent approach to executing large-scale change. This was necessary for us and will be necessary for you, given the technological disruption we are experiencing as an industry as a whole. The wholesale change that happened at our firm was one of shifting from an inwardly focused environment to an outwardly focused, client-centric environment.

Your new village will not spring into existence on its own. You need to unleash a strong force to push the innovation needed in your company. Do not shy away from repurposing and redefining existing roles in your firm. Make sure you have people in positions who can address the needs of today's clients, and make sure those people have the natural talent and are properly trained for those roles.

Violent Leadership is about change and innovation. Be the disruptive force in your profession or industry. Be proactive with the technological disruption. Adapt and change before you are left behind.

CHAPTER 7

CREATING A COOL CULTURE

ESTABLISHING CULTURE WITHIN A company starts with the leader and trickles down. The thermostat in your firm needs to set the tone and the culture within the firm. This is something about Violent Leadership that I learned the hard way.

When Stan and I made the leap from our former company to MRZ today, it was because we simply could not get up every morning and go to the organization and love being there. As soon as the day was over, we could not wait to get out.

We were caught in a closed culture. Everything was closed off. There were larger offices that each had two or three people in them rather than working in an open floor plan. The arrangement did not create an opportunity for dialogue and interaction and collaboration, and this meant there was no working theory of teamwork. Partners were more concerned about their personal wealth than they were about delivering a good service to the client. The client experience was not a factor. The partners' focus was "How much money can we make and how much can we take out?" They did that very well.

Our team there tried to focus on the client and on teamwork. One day out of each week, we gathered in my office for a social hour that was an opportunity for the team to talk and interact with the managing partner and leaders. Jon Meadows, one of my partners, spearheaded this. He would go around the firm and specifically invite people: "Hey, why don't you hang out with us this afternoon at five?" The staff members were surprised. "We are invited to that?" It was very unusual to be invited anywhere.

Except for this one social hour each week, once 5 p.m. hit, everyone took off in different directions. They would get in early, keep their heads down, and leave on the dot at five.

As partners and leaders, we were not allowed to have our own ideas and our own freedoms. For example, on a day we had a tax deadline, our tax processor, the one who handled all of our tax return processing, had to get twenty-five tax returns filed. At 7 p.m., her head was down as she focused on this important task. There had been a lunch that day, and the lunchroom had not been cleaned up—her responsibility. Knowing the importance of her tasks, Stan jumped in and told her he would take care of it so that she could stay there and finish the tax returns and we could all leave the office sooner. Another partner overheard this and reprimanded Stan on the spot. "That's her job," he said. "She needs to get in here and get that cleaned up. She can stay here tonight and get that done."

This, of course, did not fit our attitude of team play, of jumping in to get things done. The lack of teamwork, collaboration, fun, energy, and passion was toxic. The firm was in a great location. It looked nice. The people were smart. They made a lot of money, but the culture itself was not conducive to enjoying work.

Stan reached his limit. He knew I had, too. He could tell there was a lot of conflict between me and the other partners.

"Something's got to give," Stan said. We knew what we didn't want, and now it was time to decide what we *did* want. That change was going to require setting up a new firm. Together, Stan, James, and I gave our notice.

We knew we wanted to be in a place where, once our feet hit the floor every morning, we could not wait to get to the office and engage with the people there. We wanted to enjoy our working hours and be passionate about our work. We wanted to work hard but have fun doing it.

We resolved to create a place where everyone could work hard and have fun, where turnover was nonexistent because the energy and engagement in the workplace kept everyone motivated and driven.

We knew that this would have to start with us. It would not leap into existence just because we said so. We knew that we had to lead the way. We had to have the passion and energy to set the tone, and we had to hire the right people who would pick it up and run with it. We knew we needed to develop a specific kind of culture and develop the people within that atmosphere. Most importantly, we needed to put our words into action and adopt practices that would foster the kind of environment we envisioned. We resolved that we would not just have a good culture, we would have a *great* culture.

As with all proactive practices of Violent Leadership, we did not leave our company's culture to chance. It had to be intentional. We had seen how partners' actions reflect in the behavior of staff. Therefore, we were intentional, strategic. We gave it a lot of thought, to both define and introduce practices to manifest a cool culture on a daily basis. Every action we took, every word we spoke, every decision we made was to create our culture. It was the primary focus of our organization.

Because we had to find new offices, we deliberately chose something open that would foster collaboration. We chose a wide-open, bullpen-type floor plan with no cubicles. We opted for clean, contemporary, modern paint, something that made us feel good to be there. It was very important for us to have the aesthetic right.

We chose furniture that did not form walls. Everything was low. I could have privacy but still look across the room at eye level and see everybody. This fostered open dialogue and collaboration. It allowed people to interact with each other and create a team atmosphere. The office itself was an integral part of creating our cool culture.

Even making coffee became part of our culture. I used to stop at Starbucks every morning, as did many staff members, and it occurred to me that we should have a Starbucks bar at the office. We rejected the old system of pouring cheap coffee into an urn to make a brew that is undrinkable after a few hours. We went out and bought a Keurig machine and filled it with Starbucks, and every week, I stopped by the grocery store for real half-and-half creamer. Today that tradition continues. In fact, one staff member commented that this was one of the first things she noticed about our partners setting the tone for our culture: no one ever said, "That is not my job, you do it." She noticed that we set the tone of team play that others followed. We were willing to do what the organization needed, even if it meant grabbing some creamer. It helped to nurture and support our environment.

The morning coffee experience is an important detail in getting the day started. It was not cheap, but it encouraged people to come to the office before they went anywhere else. They got their day off to a good start, and they got to know their colleagues.

We added weekly events that had a social element. Every Thursday at 4 p.m., we would get together and do something: chatting in my office or heading to a local restaurant for a social hour. It was a great way to foster interactivity.

We had already added a pool table that our employees loved when Lawrence, a young staff person in the office, came to us with a chart and a pitch to get us to buy a Golden Tee machine. We didn't know what it was, but it is a popular arcade game with millennials. He created a chart of people's efficiencies and satisfaction. Somewhere on the chart, he showed us where staff satisfaction was before we bought the Golden Tee machine and projected that to a future date after we had bought the machine. It was not real data, but we had to hand it to him for creatively thinking his presentation through. His point was "If you guys will make this investment in this, our morale, satisfaction, and efficiency is going to go through the roof."

We had to support it because we were impressed by his diligence and passion. We did not really have the $3,000 to spare at the time to buy the machine, but we did it anyway. He was right. When people were done in the evening, they did not want to leave our office.

There was another young man in our office whom I saw every night when I worked late. When it is not tax season, mostly everyone is gone by 8 p.m. Nevertheless, I kept seeing this young man there every night. It was not busy season, so there was no pressure at that time. Finally, I asked someone about him and was told that he was studying for his CPA exams and he preferred to study at the office. It was quiet, and he had coffee, water, resources, better Internet, and a better all-round atmosphere in which to study than he did at home.

It was gratifying to see. We had created a place where people wanted to be. If we had sleep pods, some people would sleep here. It is that great a place.

INGREDIENTS OF A COOL CULTURE

Creating a cool culture takes focus and effort. It requires listening not only to ideas but also to criticism and feedback. It is a perfect recipe of what I call the Five Ps of culture: people, passion, purpose, practices, and place.

People

In his book *Good to Great: Why Some Companies Make the Leap … And Others Don't,*[10] Jim Collins writes, "It's not just about having the people on the bus. You've got to have the right people on the bus in the right seats." This means the first order of business is hiring people who fit the culture.

Before we talk about a candidate's skills, they have to pass the culture test. We do personality assessments to see how they interact with others. If they do not fit in with the others, we will not take a chance on them. It is easier to train someone in the skill set we need than it is to change their attitude if they are just not a good fit personality-wise. We do not just need talent—we need the right talent.

Managing the Person

Everybody is different. Everybody has different circumstances in their life, which means our policies do not fit everybody all the time. Therefore, we adapt to the person. The wife of our employee John

---

10   Jim Collins, *Good to Great: Why Some Companies Make the Leap...And Others Don't* (New York: HarperBusiness, 2001).

Helton was having complications with twins in her third trimester. He was the only one able to care for her. Our paid time off wasn't intended for taking three solid months off, but we saw his situation, so we approached him and said, "You go take care for your wife. We're going to keep paying you. Now, it is not free. You are going to make it up to us, but we are going to work with you." We ended up setting him up with a computer in the hospital so that he could do what he needed to do for us and for her. That was a case of recognizing that we needed to manage a person, not a workforce. For us, rules are guidelines; they are not meant to be hard and fast.

Fostering a Culture of Ideas

Some of our best ideas come from the youngest people. This is why we listen. People ask me how we came so far in such a short time, and I say, "I just listened and acted on what I heard." The reason we have Bring Your Dog to Work Day and casual dress is because we listened to someone when they made a suggestion. These simple, special ideas have a remarkable effect on morale. In fact, casual dress is a policy now, not just a once-a-week occasion.

When we want something to be innovative, we get together as a group. If someone has a great idea, we want to hear about it, so we introduced what we call "rollout days," where we get the whole firm together for a day and vision cast. We remind people of our culture, and we talk about our vision for the upcoming year. It is a whole day of empowering and motivating staff to really roll out their vision for the next year.

During the rollout, I teach the new people about culture in their first year with us. I explain how important each of them is to the firm and how important we feel it is to have great people here. "Hey, you know what, guys, here's our philosophy: We're on this bus together.

It's the good to great model. We've got everybody on the bus. And you should all be in the right seats going in the right direction." However, I also explain the opposite: if we decide you do not belong on the bus, we will stop the bus and let you off.

We also have smaller rollouts. We are just about to start getting together with a certain age group—the younger employees, the millennials. There is no agenda. We are just going to have idea sessions where there are no bad ideas—there are just ideas to get the brainstorm started.

We also have rollouts for our partners, where only the partners get together, and they do the same thing. There is no agenda; we just show up with sticky notes and memo pads and stick ideas on the wall as they emerge. This creates an atmosphere that supports fantastic brainstorming and ultimately a host of new ideas.

Passion

Passion is best when combined with purpose—to be enthused and motivated every day, you need passion as well as purpose, or the belief that what you are doing matters—but I'll talk about that a little later.

Passion starts at the top. If I walk around the office with the passion and energy of Violent Leadership, it affects the rest of the office. If you are going to imbue passion and energy in your firm, someone has to walk around interacting with people with a sense of urgency, a dynamic tone of voice, and an attitude that is infectious. It does not have to be only one leader—it can be all leaders. Many people have told me, "Wes, wow, what you all are doing is infectious."

In turn, sensing the passion and motivation when you walk around the office is exciting. People care about what they are doing and this translates into a quality result and great client care.

Purpose

Those of the millennial generation who joined our firm deserve a lot of credit for imbuing a sense of purpose in our culture. They are very purpose focused (see more on this in chapter 9). If it had not been for their drive to have a sense of purpose in everything they do, we might not have defined this as part of our culture. It was in defining purpose that everyone gained a heightened sense that what they do matters to people.

While speaking at several conferences for CPAs, I often ask the audience, "What is your purpose?" Typically, about 90 percent will respond, "Our purpose is to prepare tax returns and audits and financial statements." My response is to tell them that is not their purpose. If they are going to engage and retain the next generation, they need to rethink the concept of purpose, and that concept needs to include impacting the lives of employees, clients, and community. In fact, everything they do needs to revolve around that.

Tax returns are a byproduct. What we do is provide ideas, answers, and results for our clients. Our purpose is to make our clients' lives better. This is why we need to be clear on our purpose. We need to recognize that there's more to this than just being a book-keeper or a tax return preparer. Each employee needs to feel they have a purpose here.

At MRZ, this shows in our community efforts. We do not have to beg our people to do something in the community. They line up asking what they can do because they know they can have an impact on the community. I believe the loyalty we have and the reason we have such low staff turnover is that people have engaged with what matters and know they have a purpose.

At Royalwood Church, where my family and I are active members, we bought five hundred backpacks for kids who could not afford them and bought all the school supplies they needed to go in them. There were boxes and boxes of school supplies and backpacks. However, someone had to stuff them: five hundred pens, pencils, paper, crayons, and other supplies had to be put into five hundred backpacks and be ready to be given out the next day, which was Saturday.

I sent an email to the firm. I knew it was a lot to ask them to give up their Friday night on short notice to stuff backpacks. I told them not to worry if they could not do it. However, I had an overwhelming response from our people. More people from our firm showed up than from any other organization. This is because we fostered a sense of purpose and they all dialed into it. For them, it was an opportunity to help someone else.

A purpose-driven organization has more loyalty and more effectiveness than one that does not. As accountants, we think our product is our purpose, but our product and service is not our purpose. People are our purpose.

Practices

Certain practices support our culture. In addition to those discussed previously, such as paid time off and openness in physicality and attitude, we also include transparency, onboarding, technology or a home setup for everybody, no criticism without solution, an open path to partner, and providing termination announcements.

Transparency

At MRZ, we believe that transparency fosters trust. Practicing transparency is a key component of our culture, so in our second year of business we rented out a theater and gathered everyone in the room to watch a series of presentations from various people in the firm. Throughout the day, we did some fun stuff; we ate together and mingled and chatted with each other. It was an opportunity to get in front of the entire firm and share the vision and direction we were going.

We decided to do this every year with a theme. This year, the theme was purpose. Each partner got up and shared a fifteen- to twenty-minute story about purpose and what it meant to them. They personalized it. This produced some great stories. It was a profound way to share, and some people were moved to tears.

Stan's story was about how important the firm was to his family and how providing for his two young daughters gave him a purpose in coming to work everyday. At the same time, the flexibility of MRZ allowed him not only to provide financially but also to spend time with them. His story, told from a family perspective, showed how the elements of our culture and our emphasis on supporting people's purpose made his family life better.

Onboarding

Training, especially for onboarding, is an important aspect of fostering our cool culture. We provide a focused two-week process of individualized training in our technology and software, and we have each new person shadow a more senior staff person for the whole two weeks. Our onboarding process is well thought through.

By utilizing BambooHR.com, our process is paperless and streamlined. By streamlining boring legal and employment docs, we can fast-forward to the cool stuff. Onboarding should not be just about paperwork anymore; it should be about connecting with your new employee and allowing them to learn as much about you as possible. Ninety percent of employees decide whether to stay or go within the first six months of employment.

Part of this training is culture training, not only to introduce the benefits and all the great things about our culture but also to introduce the unwritten rules, such as respecting people's time and being mindful not to bother others as people walk around the open office. Our culture training is incredibly important, because it sets the tone and our expectation for employees' behavior from day one. In this way, we can convey how we expect new people to talk and interact. We show them the benefits of the company, what we offer, and what their responsibilities are.

The new hire is welcomed with a share of the MRZ swag (backpack, padfolio, tumbler, shirts, etc.) right away so that they feel as if they are a part of the team immediately. We gather the whole firm together to toast and welcome the new hire on the first day in order to make them feel welcome to our firm.

After ninety days, we follow up with them regarding their experience to find out what is working and what is not. We believe it is incredibly important for a long-term career with us that we are meeting each other's expectations. Internally, it also allows us to measure how effectively we are working to get the new hire onboard.

Technology

Technology is an important part of our culture. It says we are leading, we are cutting edge, we are on top of things, and we are not old school. Therefore, we put a lot of effort and money into technology, because it attracts and retains talent and creates a culture of efficiency in our firm. This means having setups where everyone has three to five monitors on their desk and a laptop with the tools they need to sit at their space and be efficient.

We also use technology to ensure flexibility. We set people up at home. We put in a docking station and give them two monitors and a laptop so they can work in both places. If an employee has small children and has to go home at 5 p.m. to feed them, bathe them, and get them to bed, and they still have a lot of work to do, they can be back online at 8 p.m. when their children are sleeping.

This flexibility attracted Steve Elliott, who had three nine-year-old daughters, to our firm. A week after his initial start date, we set him up with a wireless work alternative from home, including three screens and related equipment, comparable to his MRZ office setup. Although this had been promised to him at previous firms, he never truly had a home office. During busy seasons, Steve works from home every Saturday to allow him to see his family. He is also able to work from home when he needs to keep medical appointments or attend school events. Steve says, "I don't feel the pressure or constraint that I had with other firms to be present in the office between set times each day. I love that MRZ gives me the flexibility and resources I need to be efficient and experience my family, while at the same time saving two hours of driving during rush hour traffic."

Technology also allows us to track accountability and productivity. Our sales team is accountable with SalesForce tracking. Who did they visit? Who did they win? Who did they lose? Do they have good referral sources? Our client service team is accountable with the Net Promoter Score. They also use Delighted.com to measure our effectiveness in client experience and service. Everybody's accountability is measured by technology in some way that supports our purpose in what we are doing.

From this information, we can give feedback. We can say, "Here's what you put in. Here's the result." We can see whether they are on the right path or not. This kind of feedback along the way gives them an opportunity to adjust their track rather than being told at the end of the year that they missed their goal.

Based on their performance, people are entitled to compensation. This compensation is merit based, given for work above and beyond what is expected.

Giving and Accepting Feedback

Any feedback process has the potential to be positive and negative. We tell our employees that the feedback review process should be honest. They should just tell the truth so that we can all talk about a solution.

This goes both ways. We have a rule that managers reviewing work papers from staff are not allowed to fix it for them. They give feedback and let the employee fix it themselves. It might be quicker and easier for the manager to fix it, but the hard solution of writing it down and telling the employees what they did wrong gives the employees the opportunity to correct it and learn from it.

Our culture fosters constant feedback and constant review, but this also means giving feedback on the positives. Sometimes it can take real effort to find a positive; other times we can take the positive for granted and fail to comment on it. It takes diligence and effort. We all need to walk around and get some high-fives and pats on the back.

Ultimately, we are all better for it. We have seen the results of all this effort in our culture in terms of accountability, efficiency, excellence in client service, merit-based compensation, and meeting expectations.

Termination Announcements

When we terminate people, which does not happen often, we tell the staff someone has left, but we don't just say, "Hey, so and so is not with us anymore. We wish them the best." That creates the opportunity for gossip. Instead, we explain that someone could not meet our efficiency standards or they delivered a poor product. We tell them that although we coached and developed the person, it just was not a good fit and the person is no longer with us. We do not get into details, partly because we need to be mindful of state laws, but also because we do not want to run people down or be negative. We tell the truth because we want to be transparent. This in turn fosters trust, because people know we will not lie to them.

Place

As mentioned earlier, place is also a key component of cool culture. Our offices are open plan, to encourage interaction and a sense of community and teamwork. This also creates a sense that access to leadership is possible and even encouraged.

Our new space has no doors on offices and eighteen huddle rooms. The huddle room is a private room for meetings that was designed with collaboration and technology in mind. My office has no door and a half wall, so everyone has a window seat to me.

When you step off of the elevator into our space, there is no receptionist. You walk right into our "Social Club"—the common kitchen and fun areas where we all gather to play hard.

The key component in hiring our architecture firm, PDR, was their proposal for us. During their presentation, they focused on the culture of our firm as the foundation of the architecture and design of the space. There were weeks of culture assessment and interviews with the firm. The purpose and focus of the space was to support our culture, and our culture was dictated by our Violent Leadership philosophy.

BRANDING YOUR CULTURE

As mentioned earlier, to establish a cool culture you first need to define it so that it takes on a life within the firm. We took it a step further and actually branded it. We gave it a name: #MRZCULTure. Our marketing team was tasked with not only marketing it to the outside world but marketing it internally to say, "Here's our culture."

One simple and fun way that marketing brings our culture brand to the outside world involves giving employees our own version of the foam hand with pointed finger you get at baseball games. Our foam hand is red with #MRZaroundtheworld on it, and each time an employee takes a trip, they take a photo of the hand against the scenery. The #MRZaroundtheworld hand has pointed at some of the world's most fabulous and fantastic sites. Our employees then take the photo and post it on social media. One employee took a photo of it scuba diving, and another took one to the beach and stuck it in the sand. It is fun, and it has a positive effect on employees. When people see the great places our employees get to and how their loyalty to the firm prompts them to take these photos, it shows what a great community we have. They are off on their holidays, and they still have the MRZ hand with them.

If you are wondering whether creating and branding your culture is worth the effort, I can only say that it comes down to deciding what is important to you. If you truly want to have a cool culture, you have to make it a priority. You have to make targeted efforts in everything you do.

We also have #MRZSwag. We keep a supply of branded clothing, because people here want to wear it every day. We update the swag frequently, which is fun because employees can look forward to what new thing we have this week. I walk around the office and see hoodies, sweaters, and shirts with the brand. James Zapata and I went to the Nike website and ordered shoes that are MRZ branded.

Our efforts have paid off in a workforce that is so in tune with what we do that they want to display our brand. They are proud of it. They are our best marketing people, and we empower them to tell the world.

Externally, our culture brand helps us with recruiting. The new consumer is the millennial generation, a generation that prizes purpose. To recruit this generation, you need to offer them a sense of purpose. You need to excite them into wanting to be part of what you have created. We will talk about this more in chapter 9.

Our culture also helps our clients. When a client searches for differentiators among CPA firms, they see one firm doing tax returns and then see our focus on people. They can see that we care about our people. They see that we have purpose, and they want to be part of that.

A FIVE-YEAR REVIEW

It has been five years since Stan, James, and I first came up with the idea to set up a company that put corporate culture very much front and center in how we operate. Back then, we did not necessarily know how it would work out, but looking back on it now, I can say it has definitely been a success. Our firm and our culture is still evolving, but every morning when my feet hit the floor, I cannot wait to get to the office. What is more, there are over a hundred other people who feel the same way. When I hear other companies having problems with retention, I know that we don't, because of the effort we put into developing our culture.

Our cool culture is a product of Violent Leadership, because we decided to do what others were not doing. We resolved to have hard conversations and make hard decisions, to be transparent, to listen, and to accept feedback. This is not necessarily easy, but at the end of the day, you have to take that bull by the horns and make it happen. It takes proactive, aggressive leadership. You will meet resistance and you need to push through.

Today, the attention and priority we gave to defining and branding our culture from the outset continues as our culture continues to evolve. It started with the leadership team implementing Violent Leadership philosophy, going out, and making it happen. Today, everyone supports it and follows the practices to allow our cool culture to permeate the company.

FINAL WORDS

Be the thermostat that sets the tone and culture in your firm. It isn't easy to create a cool culture. It requires your focus and effort. Listen to ideas, criticism, and feedback from your employees to perfect the Five Ps of culture: people, passion, purpose, practices, and place.

Finally, give your culture a name that employees can rally behind. Brand your company culture just like you would any other initiative in your business. Your culture is the foundation upon which the rest of your business rests; make it a priority.

CHAPTER 8

PERSONAL HOUSEKEEPING

BEFORE SETTING UP MRZ, I worked for a time with a firm in Houston and worked very closely with one of the partners there, whom I will call Phil, a very persuasive and charismatic partner. Phil had an uncanny ability to develop new client relationships and grow a practice. I have never met anyone as talented at relationship building and developing new business. The common joke around the office was that Phil could sell ice to an Eskimo.

However, the more I worked with Phil, the more I observed that he surrounded himself with people who followed his orders, did as they were told, and never questioned what he said. They were not allowed to express their own ideas or contribute to the team, which had a serious impact on motivation. In a client meeting one day, I commented on a situation, and Phil interrupted me. He asked the client to excuse me, as I simply did not know what I was talking about. Not only was I embarrassed, I became unmotivated and disengaged. I quickly learned that if you did not do what Phil said, when he said it, and in the manner he said it, he had no use for you.

While Phil had the talent to grow a firm in a way that no one else had done before, he got in his own way and hindered both his own growth and the growth of the firm.

Phil did teach me one lesson: to do things differently. I learned from that experience to surround myself with people smarter than me and people who would minimize my weaknesses. I learned that building the team around me and leveraging their talent would allow me to grow exponentially.

When we founded MRZ, I resolved to encourage people around me and to develop others. I resolved to surround myself with smart people and allow them to be innovative and expansive and bring things to the table that we could all brainstorm about together. This meant that I needed to be willing to admit that I could not do everything; I was not perfect. I knew I needed to acknowledge my flaws and work on them instead of fearing I would look weak. The Violent Leader in me knew that being able to acknowledge my weaknesses was actually a strength, because it allowed me to build a strong team that could compensate for them and vice versa. I knew we could build out the company with that sort of culture.

However, I soon learned there was more to getting out of my own way than just doing things differently, or being open and collaborative, or not imitating someone else. I had my own habit that threatened to derail the firm's growth. The habit was the very thing I laud—my passion. Left unchecked, it turned out to have negative consequences. Oddly enough, it was my strength that was getting in my way. It was the words of Bill Reeb, a well-known author and a CPA consultant at our firm, which still ring in my ears today.

"Wes, you are a passionate guy with the incredible potential to effect change," he said. "If you don't learn to channel that passion into productive channels, it will be your downfall." That was the beginning of the evolution that changed me.

PERSONAL GROWTH

Many experiences can contribute to our personal growth. In setting up a firm, I discovered a variety of areas that demanded I grow to bring about the synergy and culture I envisioned for MRZ. These included finding a balanced way to communicate, actively listening to other people, and being willing to identify and own my own weaknesses. It was a painful path of personal growth.

Passion with Composure

One day, I was in a partner meeting with ten or twelve other partners discussing our strategy and direction. Everyone had some thoughts and ideas, as did I. However, I felt very, very strongly about mine. In my mind, I could see where we needed to be six months down the road. I saw that if we could shift the traditional approach from individual goals, objectives, wants, needs, and desires and work together as a single firm instead of a firm of individuals, we could grow rapidly.

This is not the way a CPA firm typically runs. I could see the potential in changing the status quo, but the other partners could not. The more I tried to explain, and the more I got blank stares, the more frustrated I got. Why could they not see what I saw? My response was to become more passionate, and my nascent Violent Leadership style turned negative, like a thunderstorm brewing.

Of course, I was proud of my passion, so I did not see it as a hindrance, but the fact was, I was not properly channeling my energy and eagerness to take action. Eventually, Stan took me aside. "Wes, we see how things are today," he said, "but we don't see what you see six months down the road, so your message is that we're stupid because we don't see what you see. Your demeanor is telling us that we're not as smart as you."

He showed me that instead of leading the partners step-by-step, piece-by-piece, I was throwing everything at them at once and was baffled that they could not see the potential I saw, and then I gave them the impression that they were stupid because they did not get it. My own inability to communicate my passion and vision effectively meant I was getting in my own way. I realized I did not have the communication skills to convey ideas in a way that people could actually follow, and my tone was turning them off. I could have great ideas, but they were not listening. What I needed to do was stop and admit, "Wait, Wes. You were the one with the communication problem. You need to calm down, take a deep breath, and lead them along one little piece at a time. Don't make them feel stupid or inferior. They just cannot see what you see right now. But they can, and when they do, they will follow you."

It was a hard lesson to look at the traits I am proud of—my vision and passion—and realize that I was using them in a way that was hurting myself and the partners and my firm. I had to learn that no matter what I brought to the table, it did not give me a free pass to talk or act however I wanted. This was a wake-up call that demanded I do some self-reflection. I had to learn to turn my ideas into effective actions, to execute my ideas in smaller pieces so that people could digest them. Instead of rushing people a hundred miles in one go, I had to lead them one mile at a time.

We often let our egos get in the way of self-questioning and personal responsibility. That experience taught me, anytime I have conflict, to take a close look at myself and ask, "What is it I need to do better to communicate, convey my ideas, help explain what I'm feeling, thinking, seeing in a better way?" This is a key component of Violent Leadership philosophy—to constantly be improving and questioning not only our firm's policies but also ourselves and our own actions. Not accepting the status quo also applies to us as individuals. We have to be proactive about our own personal growth; after all, as the saying goes, "you never stop learning."

As a leader, I had to learn that passion without composure is ineffective. While passion and energy excites people and motivates them, it can become an angry and negative force if not channeled properly. Composure, on the other hand, builds trust. Learning to do this naturally required a considerable amount of personal growth. This evolution has not only allowed me to better channel my passion, it has also allowed me to mentor and develop the people around me to be better communicators, developers of people, and agents for positive change.

Listening Is Hard

I learned that listening is hard the hard way when a company came to meet us as potential CPAs for their business. They met with Evan Tierce, our practice growth partner, and me. They had already shared their historical information with us prior to the meeting. When I read the information, I already came to a conclusion; what they needed to do was obvious to me.

I was so excited about what I had found and the savings we could make for them that I took the conversation down the path of what they needed to do. I felt my role was to provide answers, so I presented them with actions and solutions. In hindsight, I realized that I led that entire conversation. I was right and I was energetic and positive about it. It was a great meeting. We shook hands, and I looked at Evan as if to say, "We just knocked that out of the park!" As if we had solved world peace.

About a week later, Evan told me that we lost their account to a competitor. I could not fathom how that was possible. We could not have done better in that meeting. However, they explained to Evan that while they were grateful for the energy and the discussion, the other firm probed, asked questions, and engaged with them on where they were, their processes, and how they felt about them. That firm came to the same conclusion that we did. The difference was that they listened to the client's needs, concerns, and wants rather than just looking at the numbers and throwing a solution at them.

I learned that day that listening is hard. We all have our ideas. We like to talk about ourselves and about our ideas. We like to share them. This means that we can quite often forget to listen. I often find myself wanting to tell stories more than actively listen to others' stories.

Active listening is the act of mindfully hearing and attempting to comprehend the meaning of words spoken by another in a conversation or speech.[11] It is not listening to figure out what to say next, and it is not listening to fix them. It is not about giving instruction or telling them what to do. Saying, "Hey, I want to help you. I want to fix that. I want to make it better, so I'm going to give instruction. I want to move you down the road" is not active listening.

When you have an impulse to fix things and forge ahead, it can be hard to just stop and ask questions and listen without sharing opinions, but this is exactly what you need to do.

---

11   *Business Directory*. WebFinance Inc. 2017. Available at http://www.businessdic-tionary.com/definition/active-listening.html.

Active listening is listening to what is important to the other person. It means repeating back to someone what you heard them say. As an active listening leader, taking notes tells someone, "Hey, I'm listening. What you are saying is important." That is Violent Leadership; it demands you be active by asking questions, listening to the response, and taking notes.

That client would have been a big account for us to land, but we didn't win it, because I wasn't listening. I was too busy talking, telling the story, and "helping them." They acknowledged that, but I learned that day that I had to listen and not just talk—even if I did believe I had the best solution for them.

It is important to remember as a leader that you show you care by expressing interest and by just listening. If you are not particularly empathetic and do not connect easily, then active listening is essential. That is where Violent Leadership comes into play. You do not just sit and let them talk—you ask questions, you draw them out. You ask why, and you let the conversation evolve organically from there. It just shows that you care, are interested, and want to hear what they have to say.

These days when I have a meeting with a potential new client, I prepare about five questions beforehand. If the clients are slow to talk about themselves, I can use the questions to get them to open up. I follow up each answer with open questions, such as "what …?" or "why…?" because this always leads to more information. If I find that I have to ask "why" multiple times on the same subject or same point, I can get to what they really want to talk about. Finally, I repeat back to them what I believe they said, "This is what I've heard you say. Is that correct?" I've found in all relationships that this is important. I cannot assume that I have heard and understood correctly. That is active listening.

No Progress without Pain

Sometimes there is a place of brokenness and humbleness in pain that leads you to tears. Becoming a Violent Leader, creating a culture I had long envisioned, demanded I grow as a person. That growth was often painful. Sometimes the demands of business, coupled with the humility of learning hard lessons, became overwhelming. I had to listen to some harsh truths without getting defensive. Sometimes it took a few knocks before my ego got out of the way and I was humbled enough to listen. It can be very difficult to listen to other people mirroring our shortcomings.

I knew I had to be willing to listen to people I trusted when they were giving me feedback. I had to learn to recognize the difference between people who were just critical and people who were offering constructive criticism. Sometimes, however, the people closest to you, the ones you trust most, give you the harshest feedback. There were some weekends when I left the office feeling bruised and beaten up.

My first instinct was to push back and be angry and defensive. Today, when I find myself being defensive, I stop and consider the situation and my role in it. That is what this style of leadership makes you do. You look at yourself and decide that you cannot be that way. Defensiveness is not productive. Some mechanism needs to be found so that when something is triggered, your response is to step back, decompress, and return with clarity.

Finding a safe place to release frustration—and passion, and pain, and emotion—is important. I needed a place I could go to help me cope and rally so that I could continue the hard path to manifest my vision, because I knew in the end there could be no gain without pain. For me, that place is my faith. I can go to church for a few hours of worship. There I can find a place where it is dark and quiet and feel I am alone with God. It is an emotionally safe place. It is a place where one of my greatest mentors, Pastor Ron Macey, speaks from a pulpit directly to me. It gives me the opportunity to let it all out, the frustration and the tears, and hit the bottom. Then from that place, I can find the solace, quiet, and peace I need to hit the reset button and stand up with new energy.

Whether it is prayer, contemplation, counseling, or yoga—whatever helps you find that individual, quiet, one-on-one time to decompress and reset—finding a place that allows you to get up again on Monday to do it again, only better, is key. It makes it possible to take feedback or criticism and, instead of lashing out on the defensive and escalating conflict, turn it into a learning and growth opportunity. The important thing is that you find a safe place to reflect and recuperate from the sting of criticisms in order to discern what is useful and what you need to take ownership of, and reject what is not useful. That place of brokenness, pain, and humility is good. It allows you to get your ego and even perhaps self-pity out of the way so that you can be an effective leader. That place can be a good place to visit every now and then, because it keeps our ego in check and heals whatever obstacles we have put in our own way.

PERSONAL PRODUCTIVITY

My faith kept me in check, tempered my emotions, and gave me a sense of purpose and direction. My belief in a higher power gave me purpose and serenity. While this was the most important part of my life, I found that there were practices and habits that supported this foundation. Violent Leadership did not only mean being consistent and intentional about my faith, it also extended to taking a proactive role in my everyday life. Maintaining a healthy space for myself also meant finding a physical space with the right people, partners, and clients that occupy it. Importantly, this space also needs to be decluttered.

Decluttering

Decluttering your world is important for productivity. This means getting rid of negative noise. It means choosing people to follow who offer sustenance and useful advice and information. It means creating the space to discern between people who are actually good for you and people who are just being negative and critical. It allows you to assess whether your business relationships are right for you and which clients you should be keeping and which clients you should be cutting loose.

Violent Leadership calls for an intentional effort in all these areas. This comes into play when you are looking for people to work with on your team. Many people look for others who make them feel better—by making them feel intellectually superior, for example—but it is better to look around for people who can compensate for your weaknesses. Look for people much stronger in those areas than you will ever be. If you are not a detail person, put people around you who are extremely detail oriented. By spending time in personal assessment, by being willing to identify your weaknesses, by decluttering your personal issues, and by decluttering people who are not bringing something of value to the table, you can succeed.

The key to successful teamwork is doing your own personal assessment and then surrounding yourself with people who can make up for your weaknesses. We cannot be intimidated by people who are better than us in some areas. We are only as good as the weakest link on our team.

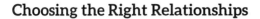

Choosing the Right Relationships

Having the right partner is an important part not only of your own personal housekeeping but can also be a key factor in the ultimate success or failure of your business.

A business relationship is almost like a marriage in that you have to be able to work together, have common goals, and have common business interests. This does not mean you have to be friends, but you need synergy and alignment if you are to work together. Your business relationships should be conducive to you growing as a Violent Leader.

For a business relationship to be healthy and productive, it is important that partners are comfortable offering feedback without fearing their head will roll because of it. A business relationship is healthy when you can get in a room, have a complete, honest, transparent, even brutal conversation, and leave any negativity behind when you walk out of the room. You need to be able to emerge positively, saying, "Here's where we are going with these ideas."

There needs to be trust in these relationships so that people can be honest with each other without fearing that any given conversation could end the relationship. When there is a high level of trust, we can each accept that we are entitled to speak up and say what we feel without repercussion. This means everyone can feel heard. It also means that situations do not escalate to a point where people need to cluster together to lead a charge against an intransigent partner. Open conversations and feedback are necessary, and these are made possible by doing personal housekeeping—by reflection, acceptance, humility, honest self-appraisal, and personal responsibility.

If you feel perpetually criticized, it is important to look at the dynamic at play. Are you being defensive? Are people just criticizing you, or are they giving you constructive feedback? The latter will come with a proposed solution, whereas critical people will say something negative without offering an actionable solution. Don't listen to those who do not have solutions. Anyone can find problems, but when someone takes the time to think through and propose a solution, that is when it is time to say, "Okay, let's talk about that." I cannot claim perfection in this area. It is one of my ongoing and consistent struggles to hear the feedback and criticism, accept it, and not be defensive.

Some conversations should only happen in person. An email is not communication; it is the transfer of information. If you need to have an emotional conversation, do it in person or over the phone where your tone can be conveyed and misinterpretation minimized. If I get an email with an emotional charge, my reply is "Hey, can we discuss?" Then I leave it alone because a battle of cluttered emails goes nowhere and certainly does not involve active listening.

Choosing the Right Clients

Some clients can bring more clutter than business to your business. There are clients who are in a state of constant conflict over fees and never get to the point of valuing your relationship. They will bring you down. It is far better to move them along and work with people who want to work with you because they value the service you offer.

Decluttering your life across the board allows you to free up time, not only for self-reflection but also to allow you the time and space to follow influencers. You may find one, two, or three people who are saying something or writing something that you can use. I always have a book in hand. Each week, I find something to read with which I can make myself a better leader.

When you declutter, you have time to devote to your own personal development. You also have time to find a mentor, formally or informally, from whom you can learn. Decluttering frees up time to find someone you want to be like or someone you can watch, follow, and draw from. You can watch what they do, how they speak, and how they comport themselves, and use that to mold something about yourself into something better.

GETTING OUT OF THE WAY

The biggest problem I see in people who want to move forward is that they get in their own way by not recognizing or owning what is wrong with them and identifying one thing they could work on. Ego can quite often inhibit self-reflection. Some people just will not listen. They will not look at themselves and see no possibility they could be wrong. They have been doing it this way for the last twenty years and see no reason for doing it differently today—they cannot envision a situation where someone else may have a better answer or a better way. However, in today's climate of globalization and rapid technological advancements, this is the surefire way to become irrelevant.

How you get in and out of your own way is unique to each individual and depends on your own characteristics and personality. It was not my nature to criticize or limit or put other people down, so I thought I could not get in my own way. In fact, if I were reading a book like this, I would have skipped this chapter. That is where hubris got in the way. It is important to recognize that we can get in our own way in a multitude of ways. To be effective leaders, we need to identify and own that, and we need to reflect and examine ourselves and our behavior if we are to change.

FINAL WORDS

Accept that you are not perfect, that there are parts of you that may be broken. If you are an overachiever, this can be a particularly hard thing to do. You need to own that and know it is okay to be flawed. Better to acknowledge your flaws and work on them than hide them for fear of being perceived as weak. Being flawed is not a sign of weakness—it's a sign of strength. It says that you are able to acknowledge your weaknesses, but because you are a Violent Leader, you refuse to accept the status quo even as it applies to you as an individual. It takes strength to take ownership of our weaknesses, but in doing that we have the greatest potential to grow.

CHAPTER 9

GENERATIONAL DISRUPTION

MANY OF US HAVE recognized the unique characteristics of the millennial generation. Born between 1980 and 2000, they are the largest generation in history and are not only filling the workforce, they are about to become the world's most important customers. They are characterized as tech centric, social online and off, collaborative, adventure seeking, and passionate about purpose.[12] They also have a tendency to distrust authority, which can make them challenging for any workplace leader.

---

12 Micah Solomon, "2015 Is the Year of the Millennial Customer: 5 Key Traits These 80 Million Consumers Share," *Forbes,* 2014. Available at https://www.forbes.com/sites/micahsolomon/2014/12/29/5-traits-that-define-the-80-million-millennial-customers-coming-your-way/#7f388b6125e5.

Millennials are bringing a generational disruption to the workplace, which makes Violent Leadership's focus on change, adaptability, and forward thinking key to remaining relevant and attractive to new talent. As a father to two millennials, I have a very distinct appreciation for the strengths and weaknesses of this generation and the role I play in empowering them.

Back in 2003, my partner James Zapata wanted to hire a twenty-seven-year-old CPA, Roger Ledbetter. Roger is an incredibly intelligent guy. He had a mortgage and a baby on the way at the time. I agreed to meet him to see if he would be a good fit for MRZ. When I met him, I sensed immediately that he was very passionate about his future and had big dreams to save the world. He was also particularly focused on his compensation. He believed he needed to be paid more because his lifestyle demanded it rather than realizing his compensation was commensurate with his performance. This was something I had noticed in many millennials—a sense of entitlement.

The idea of personal entitlement divorced from merit was an attitude inconsistent with the culture and team mentality we'd worked hard to create at MRZ, so understandably I was apprehensive about taking Roger on and incredulous that he could ever make partner.

Nevertheless, I gave him a chance. I quickly saw that he had the skill set and the manner to be a great leader. He had a polished, professional look. He had the charisma of a partner, the ability to connect with people, and he was a quick study. He was smart and knowledgeable. He had common sense beyond his age. His interpersonal skills made him a great personnel manager. People followed him. He also had great technical skills. In a very raw sense, he was a leader.

However, he lacked the entrepreneurial attitude of "I'm responsible for my own future. Nobody else is. How do I affect and change it?" He needed to learn that no one was going to hand him anything just because he thought he deserved it. He needed to learn that he needed to earn a promotion or pay increase.

Because of the potential that James and I both saw in him, we tried to mold him into our cool culture and our Violent Leadership philosophy. We knew it would take some work—that we could not just roll him into the company to be the antithesis of everything we had worked to set up within the company. First we needed to take his proactive attitude, need for purpose, and collaborative impulse and blend it with the merit-based philosophy and company-wide sense of teamwork at MRZ.

Over time, we worked with him to draw out what was best in him and knock off the "entitled" edges. The most obvious place that needed work was his attitude toward compensation. His attitude was not based on effort or personal responsibility for what he had done but on his belief that "I should get paid my salary because that's what it takes for me to live."

We told him outright that he was not going to get a pay increase based on what it takes to support his lifestyle. If he was going to get a pay increase, it would be based on merit, on what he brought to the firm. The sharpest turn Roger had to make was in the area of personal accountability.

The first and most basic lesson for Roger was the economics of how a company works. He had to understand that there was no money tree and that he had to go out and create more value for clients. When any employee does that, he or she is compensated for it. It is a basic economic model—those who generate more value, develop new business, and grow the firm are compensated more.

In assessing how much compensation he deserved, we taught him to look at how efficiently he was working and how much business he was managing rather than at how much it took to support his lifestyle. If he wanted to pull more money each month, then he had to produce it. This would become even more important if he were to become partner, because then nobody would be responsible for Roger except Roger. It took a while, but gradually he began to see how personal responsibility and accountability for his own production in the firm translated into compensation. He began to see that the path to partner was based on, among other things, billing hours and managing dollars.

Over time, we noticed a shift in his thinking. We started to hear him talk to his team in these terms. When they came to him with the attitude with which he had once come to us, he explained why reward was not based on their wants and desires but on merit.

One day Roger came to me and said, "You know what? I get this now. My team members want to make more money, but they have to do their part to earn the increase. I ask them, 'Did you put your 1,600 hours in this year? Did you do the things we asked you to do? Have you done your part to earn and deserve an increase?'"

With this realization, he recognized that if the people under him did not make money, he did not make money. As you move up, this is the way the world works. It is not just your personal effort that matters, but also the effort of the people around you. When Roger finally got this, he began to walk the path to partner.

The key to helping Roger become the best leader he could be required that we put him in a leadership role and help him to deliver. This in itself was a disruption from the traditional model of most CPA firms. People often say, "he or she is not ready," but many times people will not be ready until they are challenged with the role. This is especially important with the millennial generation. As part of the previous generation, we were more inclined to be promoted when we were ready, or when we had put in so many years. This generation is smarter and more creative and more purpose driven, so that when they are given a challenge and offered the right teaching and training and coaching, they respond very positively and excel quicker than previous generations did.

When Roger was promoted, he became our youngest partner. By most firms' standards, he was not ready, but we saw raw talent and leadership ability. We gambled that if we gave him the chance, he would step up to the plate and deliver. We were right.

Roger's story also highlights that old styles of management will not work with the millennial generation. To adapt and change and draw out the best in them, certain practices need to be adopted and adapted to your leadership in order to effectively handle the generational disruption they bring to your firm.

UNDERSTANDING THE MILLENNIAL

Every generation thinks the succeeding one has problems. Our parents looked at us as if there were something wrong with us because we were different, and our view of the millennial generation is no different. We may think that their greater interest in what is happening outside the office than what is happening inside the office is evidence that they are lazy and not particularly loyal to their employer. We may perceive them to be less career driven and more focused on work–life balance, at least in the early stages of their career. However, we need to actively listen, and observe that they bring some great attributes to the table: they are smart, social, open to feedback, and community minded, which can be great assets to your firm.

Smarts

From a technical perspective, millennials appear to be driven and prepared for their career in terms of education. They come to the workplace with a knowledge and understanding of how things work that is light-years ahead of where I was at that point in my life. They are more likely to be overachievers. What took my generation seven years in a career path to develop, they do in four or five. This means that to be an effective Violent Leader you must recognize that millennials are moving on a faster trajectory, and you need to be careful about holding them back or pacing them according to traditional HR models.

Sociability

Technology has made millennials very social online and off. They hang out and have coffee together in the mornings. We have softball teams and extracurricular sports activities for the firm, so they hang out together after work. My generation came to the office, did our work, and went home. Violent Leadership demands adjusting to this kind of sociability. Information is shared quickly, so you have to anticipate that what you say to one will be known by everyone within minutes. They disseminate information quickly and they stick together. They then bring issues to the fore as a group, not as individuals.

Their sociability also extends to a different level of social awareness. They want to take care of those around them, not just themselves. They are concerned about the greater good of their peers. That said, they do not take care of others themselves but instead will lobby for the leadership to take care of them. This means that you as a leader need to factor in their demands for fairness and equality for all concerned into account.

Openness to Feedback

The millennials I know love feedback. They challenge their managers because they want to know the "why" of everything, which means that as a Violent Leader, you cannot just give them a list of rules. They need to understand why a rule exists—the reasoning behind it.

This challenged how we did things in the office. Formerly, someone would turn a tax return into their manager, and the manager would correct the errors they found during their review of the tax return. We quickly found out that this would not work with millennials. They came to us saying they were tired of a manager correcting their errors; they wanted to know what the manager did so that they could do it themselves the next time. We had to shift gears and tell our managers to review the return, leave the feedback and review notes in the file for what needed correction, and send it back to the staff member to let them know what they did wrong. This would then allow the staff person to make the corrections and learn from the feedback how they could improve and be better.

Millennials do not want an annual review; they want reviews each step of the way. We adapted by cutting our annual review process to only about five questions, but we also do reviews on a project-by-project basis to offer suggestions for improvement. We answer their "how" and "why" on a regular basis.

Sense of Community

There is a sense of community in everything that many millennials do, to the point of being almost packlike. They want to give back, even to the community at large. If we volunteer to stuff lunch boxes for the kids of needy families, they are down there at 7:30 a.m. to help. We do not have to beg them. They want to spend their time helping others and affecting the community around them. To do them justice, they seem to want to give back more than our generation did.

WORKING WITH MILLENNIALS

Millennials are the generation of the future, which means the Violent Leader must dig a little deeper to understand where they are coming from in order to identify the management style required to bring the best out in them. What worked ten or twenty years ago will not work today. The positive attributes millennials bring to the workplace need to be tempered with the lesson the earlier generations learned at home: no reward without hard work. There are no participation trophies. Participation is expected.

WE HAVE IDENTIFIED SEVEN DIFFERENT WAYS TO APPROACH WORKING WITH MILLENNIALS:

1. Be transparent.

2. Promote them when they are ready or before they are ready.

3. Pay them according to their role.

4. Provide the latest technology.

5. Actively listen.

6. Express appreciation.

7. Hold them accountable.

The Importance of Transparency

In chapter 8, we reinforced the importance of transparency to a great culture. Transparency is not only directly tied to a great culture, it seems to be a generational expectation of millennials. In my experience, transparency is key to this generation, which seems inherently distrustful of authority. I notice they see through any form of smoke and mirrors. Try to pull the wool over their eyes to your detriment. Those in our firm have a unique ability to say, "That's not true. Don't believe that." Since trust is so important to them, to try to deceive or be secretive will do untold harm to the relationship you need to build with them. They will respect you more and value the firm more if you just tell them the truth.

When Roger came to MRZ, we were transparent every step of the way, and this helped to build trust between him and the leadership at our firm. Trust and transparency cannot be overstated when it comes to bringing a millennial into the fold. When Roger focused on what the firm could do for him instead of what he could do for the firm, we had no qualms about saying, "This is how you are behaving. This isn't going to work." He did not like it. It did not feel good to him, but his takeaway was "I trust them."

Of course, our open door policy that allows our employees to come to us with problems (as long as they have solutions) meant that feedback and open communication flowed both ways. Therefore, employees are able to see transparency permeate the office on a daily basis. In Roger's case, this helped him turn a corner. Later he said, "I can without a doubt say that what helped me convert faster was the immediacy of my interactions with those same authority figures I once so readily distrusted."

Promotion and Compensation

When it comes to promotion, millennials have a very different mentality than previous generations, and this demands a different sort of management. To truly excel, they need to be promoted when they are ready or before they are ready.

However, they are better equipped in many ways than previous generations at that age, which means we must rethink how we evaluate readiness. Traditionally, you would be a staff person for five years, a supervisor for two to five years, and a manager for at least five years, and then finally, after a minimum of fifteen years of service, you would be considered for partner. It was a very timeline-driven system. However, this generation demands we throw the timelines out in favor of milestones for action and development.

When we tell other firms that we have a thirty-year-old partner, they are astonished. Promoting Roger was a risky choice for us to make, but we trusted our instinct that while he was not ready based on experience, he was ready to grow into the position.

Promoting an employee early means being willing to spend more time developing their talent. I have found that 90 percent of those we promote are not ready, but they are ready to accept the challenge when you tell them so. We say, "You are not ready for this, but here's what you have to do to fill the shoes." They generally rise to the occasion.

Of course, promoting a thirty-year-old over a fifty-year-old who has been with us for many years is a tough conversation, and some of the latter may decide to leave. However, we have to promote with the good of the firm in mind. Just as the millennials have to learn that their compensation is based on merit, not what they think they deserve, so is promotion. The days of longevity being the key factor in promotion is long gone.

From experience, I have found that it is important not to limit this generation. If you put time constraints on their progress, they feel constrained. If you try to make them wait five or ten years for a promotion, they will go elsewhere. This means changing your overall culture and process of promotion. Being willing to accept and adapt to this disruption is made possible by the philosophy of Violent Leadership and its willingness to embrace change. These days, we simply say, "Our firm does not promote based on your time here. Promotion is merit based. We promoted x because they're more ready than you are." Our millennials certainly appreciate that bluntness, but it is important to be this direct company-wide.

Similar to the new approach to promotion, it is important to adopt a compensation system based on merit, not longevity.

Many millennials make money more quickly because they produce more efficiently. They use technology more quickly. The adage of "Okay, you are a five-year person, you should make $75,000" will not go over well today. To determine proper pay, we dig into the metrics for each individual. If they produce the same numbers as a seven-year person, they get paid the same. Our metrics are not "How long have you been here?" but "What do your numbers say you do?" Their numbers reflect their work and ability and have nothing to do with age or longevity.

Technology

We all get to a certain age where we do not adapt to technology as quickly, but millennials push it to the limit. When it comes to technology, the Violent Leader cannot afford to rest in his or her comfort zone. You must listen to them. You must provide them with the technology they want. If you do not, they will go someplace that does.

Millennials expect everything to work on their phone, so we had to start developing apps and implementing cloud technology. This served the secondary purpose of reducing paperwork. Our millennials do not like paper; they want to be paperless and able to work from the cloud anywhere. It is important, therefore, to put these systems in place and address and implement robust security measures. It is what they expect, and it means the difference between appearing innovative and archaic.

Listen

We looked at the importance of active listening company-wide earlier, but this becomes even more important with millennials. They want to engage with the firm; they want to be heard. This is part of their sociability and community mindedness. They want to be part of the community and be part of a greater purpose. You have to make time for them, and you have to actively listen.

At MRZ, we made it a policy to sit down with every millennial in our firm. There is no agenda to the meeting; we just meet and brainstorm, put ideas on sticky notes and stick them on the wall, and see where it all goes.

We implemented Bring Your Dog to Work Day based on a millennial's suggestion. I was not keen about it, but it mattered to them. Today, Bring Your Dog to Work Day has become an almost cult-like annual event that gives them all a sense of belonging to the firm. That idea came from listening to them.

Listening is one of the secrets to the success of MRZ and a key component to Violent Leadership—listening and taking action.

Accountability

One challenge presented by the millennial generation is instilling in them the philosophy that they are not automatically entitled to anything and are accountable for everything they do.

Again, it is important to stand firm on the policy of paying them according to their role and productivity. To do this effectively, the Violent Leader must set expectations from the start. We tell them that we expect so many billable hours over this period of time, and if they do not reach it, they do not get a reward. Compensation is merit based; there is no handout because they think they deserve it.

We also pull them aside if they start behaving outside what we think is the norm. We sit and have a conversation with them to set the rule for how they need to act, dress, and behave in the office.

Appreciation

We have already looked at how much the millennials on our team want feedback. This also derives from their need for recognition and appreciation. To support this, we implemented Employee of the Quarter, a recognition that is voted on by their peer group and comes with a $500 prize. We have a little ritual where everyone gathers and counts out in unison the five $100 bills. It has become a regular quarterly activity at MRZ.

We also spotlight an employee in our monthly newsletter and talk about them and their personal interests. We use these articles as tools to recognize when people excel. Every time an employee does something great or small, maybe scored a great touchdown in a game, we publish that in our newsletter and post it on social media. It is a way of celebrating and sharing their success.

Our HR onboarding process includes giving new employees a questionnaire with four or five questions about their hobbies and interests, or crazy facts about them. Then we use this information to introduce them to the firm. On their first morning we all get together with a bottle of nonalcoholic champagne and introduce and toast them: "Hey, welcome John to the firm. He likes to ski, and here's one fact about him that nobody else knows…"

We do this for people in all positions and all age groups, but the idea was proposed by a millennial. It has been a reciprocal relationship between millennials and us: we have taught them accountability and work ethic, and they have brought us a greater sense of community, technological innovation, and purpose-driven mind-set.

GET VIOLENT ABOUT CHANGE

Change is happening, whether we want it or not or like it or not. Change and disruption is a fact of life. Violent change requires Violent Leadership. The millennial generation has brought a large amount of disruption to our industry, but managed properly, it promises great change and improvement in how we do business in the future.

First, we will see more young people making partner more quickly, and they will interact better with people. This means old systems of promotion, compensation, and recognition are becoming irrelevant and need to be replaced with a merit-based, not longevity-based, structure.

Second, organizations that do not have a clear purpose or clear understanding of why they exist probably will not survive. Firms that continue to see themselves as tax preparers will become irrelevant. Providing employees with a sense that they are part of something valuable, something that has a greater purpose than themselves will become key to attraction and retention of talented people.

We will see an increase in experience-driven organizations that are focused not only on the delivery of the compliance product but also on the advisory and the consulting element of what we do, because that impacts people. Organizations will need to shift from being a very compliance-driven "you give us information and we will give you a product back" to more of an interactive advisory, client relationship-driven organization.

The biggest change we will see in our industry may well be this shift to purpose-driven service provision.

Third, millennials will continue to leverage technology and revolutionize how we deliver our services. Technology is a disruptive force in our industry, and this will continue and fundamentally change our business systems and how we perceive our role. Increasingly, technology will prepare tax returns, so we need to think in terms of providing additional value to our clients.

FINAL WORDS

To navigate the changing landscape and to effectively manage the oncoming millennial storm as a Violent Leader, you must understand that we are in an era of adapting to them just as much as we need them to adopt some of our work ethic. You need to use a style of leadership that actively owns that symbiosis and imbues that in them. Work with them, listen to them, and innovate based on their ideas instead of complaining about who they are or trying to make them do it your way.

More than ever, the proactive philosophy of Violent Leadership is key to creating a path to success in the future. Change is coming whether we want it or not. We have a lot to learn from this generation, so embrace their ideas and influence them positively. If there is one thing you learn from working with them, let it be that to be successful in the years ahead, you need to embrace this change.

CONCLUSION

In Mark 5:25–34, the Bible tells the story of a woman with a life-threatening blood disease. She had been to see doctor after doctor, but none could find a cure for her disease. She had exhausted all of her resources. The situation was hopeless. Failure after failure stared her in the face; she had heard "no cure" many times. One day, she heard that there was a man named Jesus coming to her city who was known to heal the sick. Now, whether you believe this story or not really isn't the point. To her in her desperate situation, she needed something to happen. She could easily have believed the doctors, lain down, and died of the blood disease. The day that Jesus came to her city, she went to see him, believing that if she could just get close enough to touch him, her life would be spared. As she walked into the city, she was dismayed. Thousands of people had gathered around him, and she could not even see him, much less get close enough to touch him. It was loud, hot, and crowded, with people hoping to see the celebrity who had come to the city. She was weak with her disease and could barely walk, much less force her way through the crowd. In her despair, violence gripped her heart, and she resolved to press through the crowd and through the noise to get to her goal. It was not a violence of anger or hurt, but a violence to rise up and take control of her situation and not let the circumstances and noise stand in the way of achieving her goal. With a passion to save her life, she ignored the people around her and pressed harder and harder to get to him. The story is told that she did eventually get to Jesus, was able to touch him, and was healed.

This story demonstrates the Violence necessary to overcome the noise and circumstances that stand in the way of our greatest success. Violent Leadership demands that we press through noise, negativity, popular opinions, and circumstances and lead with passion and energy. It demands that each and every time we fail, we learn from it and press on. Violent Leadership tells us that it is okay to fail and that having the courage to change is necessary.

This has been the story of my career. My journey from that little video store to running a multimillion-dollar firm has been fraught with challenges but has brought abundant rewards. There has been a lot of noise and resistance along the way. I have had to grow professionally, personally, as a leader, and then as a Violent Leader.

My journey toward Violent Leadership began with recognizing good leadership style and then—through trial and error, by following influencers, by learning what not to do from other leaders—I managed to devise and implement a new leadership style, one that challenges outmoded systems and policies and is geared for this millennium. Central to this Violent Leadership philosophy is the courage to change the status quo, the willingness to fail, and a recognition of the need to be proactive and to set the temperature of the environment.

PERSONAL GROWTH

Inspiring and influencing people to love where they work and feel part of a greater purpose in their job is a difficult task that requires a considerable amount of personal growth on the part of the Violent Leader—especially an introvert. In hindsight, I realize that a key component of being an effective leader is not just your skills as a leader, or managing people, or being a great CPA. It is your willingness to accept criticism without being defensive and the courage to identify and own and heal parts of yourself that you are not proud of or weaknesses you wish you did not have. You need to be willing to be humble and vulnerable, and recognize and own your weaknesses if you are ever to be able to overcome them to make yourself a more effective leader. You need to get out of your own way in order to lead the firm forward instead of tripping it up. Part of this road involves learning to choose the right hat—to take on a role that demands your strengths and allows you to surround yourself with people who have the right skills and attitudes to compensate for your weaknesses. Identifying and owning your own weaknesses is a key component of effective Violent Leadership. My willingness to fail made me vulnerable to those around me, but I understood that without this willingness, even with the lessons learned from failures, I was probably not going to get to my destination. In anything we do, there are going to be failures. Being willing to allow those to happen is part of being a Violent Leader.

Violent Leadership became a style that demanded a lot of courage to step out and be different. It required me to make unpopular decisions, decisions that were contrary to accepted tenets of our industry. Every time I was told I was wrong, I had to stand firm for what I believed in and navigate it though all the noise and naysayers along the way.

What has kept me going along the way and what has kept me focused is a piece of scripture that reminds me that being passive, giving up, or just letting things happen to me is not the path to success. At every step, I knew that I had to be active. I had to take control of every situation and drive the result home each time. I had to be the catalyst, the thermostat; I had to either cause to happen or create the circumstances that led me to where I wanted to go. Nothing was going to happen just because I kept my head down or because I was a good person.

Violent Leadership has made me a better leader by forcing me to look inward, self-reflect, own my weaknesses and strengthen or compensate for them, and then emerge stronger. It has allowed me to channel my passions and energy and remain focused along my path to success. Aside from my own personal and professional growth, I have seen people around me grow and be successful.

GROWING A VILLAGE

For you as a Violent Leader, putting people who are passionate about a position that utilizes their talents fosters a teamwork mentality and a synergy between all employees that can turn your firm from the old model of lots of individuals under one firm to one huge team under one roof. This allows you to create a village, not a firm, and implement a perfect division of labor that plays to the strengths of each individual. The result is increased motivation across the firm and eagerness on the part of each individual to bring something to the table.

Putting the right people in the right place comes more naturally when you intentionally create a culture that is focused on growing a village. Certainly, devising strategies and ideas to foster this culture, and making sure it was defined and understood and something your employees are proud of, is likely to be one of the more enjoyable aspects of developing as a Violent Leader and implementing Violent Leadership style.

Naturally, these cultural changes will not happen overnight, but having a clear process for onboarding staff helps. When considering implementing the Violent Leadership style, it is important to be transparent in all processes. We defined our culture, and we were clear about who we were and what we expected from our employees. We expected them to do more than their job; we expected them to bring a certain energetic attitude to the table that fit in with the climate in our company overall. In fact, our HR process diverged from the traditional process. We prioritized personality. Skills we can teach, attitude we can influence, but we cannot change a personality. This process has stood the test of time.

Our HR processes and our focus on culture, innovation, and providing value added to our clients has melded together to enhance my original aspirations for our firm's culture. Today we are team- and community-focused. Our employees value opportunities to give back—to look out for others and help the community at large. There is passion in our employees—passion for their jobs, for their role and purpose in the firm, and for their ability to contribute to the community at large. This is all the result of Violent Leadership.

To affect people around you, you need to be able to bring your passion to work. You need to use your passion—the way you act and the energy you exude—to get people excited. If you want to groom better leaders, you not only need to lead people somewhere, you also need to impact them. You need to encourage them, not limit them. You must actively listen to make sure your staff members feel that what they have to say matters and that they are valued members of your team.

You need them to be strong, because you need to surround yourself with people who are strong in areas where you are weak. This is also a characteristic of Violent Leadership. It is strong and courageous and yet vulnerable and honest. It builds people up, and it cares about people. In turn, people care about you. When this happens, you have created the perfect village.

FACING FORWARD

The face of our industry has been changing under our noses, and this change is going to accelerate. Violent Leadership skills are truly honed when looking forward into the future. The seeds of where our industry will be in five or ten years are already planted. We see it daily with the millennial generation. More than ever, we are seeing that traditional ways of operating no longer work. The younger generation is changing the status quo. Not only is having partners working to bring in sales an ineffective way to operate, but soon, having a firm of partners working as individuals looking out for their own interests will become irrelevant in a generation that is marked by community and collaborative spirit. Today, firms need to restructure to put in place a focused and combined effort to move the firm forward.

This focus on purpose and fulfillment is endemic in modern culture and therefore needs to be adopted within our corporate culture. Millennials are not only our employees, they are our customers. Their characteristics of sociability, upward mobility, disruption and innovation, and community mindeness now exists on both sides of the table. We need to adjust our language and our attitude if we are to attract them as employees and as clients.

Externally, this means that we can no longer perceive ourselves as a tax return preparation industry. Technology demands that we offer a personal touch to show clients they are being listened to—and provided solutions tailored to their wants and desires and where they want to be.

Internally, we need to shift our attitudes in the direction of merit-based compensation and promotion, openness and transparency, and technological innovation, as well as our attitudes toward engaging and appreciating rather than dictating. The people filling the ranks of our firms are hungry for change, and the ability of Violent Leadership to anticipate and embrace change makes it the optimum leadership style of the future.

BE THE CHANGE

Essentially, Violent Leadership means taking things by force. Success comes by doing something, not by waiting for something to happen. It is a hands-on style of leadership. It is proactive, not reactive. It does not react to change; it *is* the change. The Violent Leader causes the disruption. It works because it does not accept the status quo.

Change and disruption is a fact of life. To stay relevant, you need to decide whether you are going to be swept away in the tornado or be part of the force as it sweeps through our profession. If you are not the latter, you will be the next Blockbuster or the next company that no longer exists.

The surest way to survive our current business climate is to adopt the Violent Leadership style. It will allow you to push through the noise and disruption and stand up as a leader—and not just any leader but a better leader. Remember, you are master of your own fate. If you take one or two chapters from this book and execute them one at a time in your life, you will see the positive impact they will have on you and the people around you. They will make you stronger, and they will keep you relevant in the years ahead.

OUR AWARDS

IPA Top 300 Firms

August 2017—*INSIDE Public Accounting*

IPA compiles lists and statistical data of top accounting firms in the United States. Top 300 firms are recognized annually.

C-Suite Award Finalist

July 2017—*Houston Business Journal*

Annual award for Outstanding CEO of 2017—Wesley Middleton, Managing Partner, MRZ LLP.

Houston's 2017 Best and Brightest Companies to Work For

March 2017—The National Association for Business Resources

The Best and Brightest Companies to Work For® competition identifies and honors organizations that display a commitment to excellence in their human resource practices and employee enrichment.

Organizations are assessed based on categories such as communication, work-life balance, employee education, diversity, recognition, retention, and more. All participating companies receive a complimentary assessment report and benefits throughout the year. Winning companies are invited to celebrate in one of our many event regions.

2016 Fastest Growing Firms
October 2016—*INSIDE Public Accounting*
IPA ranks fastest-growing firms by organic growth, which is the percentage of growth in net revenues from the previous year excluding mergers and acquisitions. The data is also displayed by region, and all the graphs and analysis will be available in the October issue of *INSIDE Public Accounting*.

HBJ Best Places to Work (#1)
October 2016—*Houston Business Journal*
The HBJ Best Places to Work lists are compiled by Quantum Workplace, which sent a survey to employees of nominated companies. Quantum then compiled scores based on corporate culture, amenities, benefits, and worker retention and attraction strategies.

Best Accounting Firms to Work For
August 2016—*Accounting Today*
The annual survey and awards program, which is conducted in partnership with Best Companies Group, is designed to identify, recognize, and honor the best employers in the accounting profession, benefiting its economy, workforce, and businesses.

Houston's 2016 Best and Brightest Companies to Work For
March 2016—The National Association for Business Resources

2015 Fastest Growing Firms (#1)

October 2015—*INSIDE Public Accounting*

HBJ Best Places to Work (#1)

October 2015—*Houston Business Journal*

Houston's 2015 Best and Brightest Companies to Work For

March 2015—The National Association of Business Resources

HBJ Best Places to Work (#29)

October 2014—*Houston Business Journal*

Best Accounting Firms to Work For

August 2014—*Accounting Today*

APPENDIX B

RECOMMENDED READING

Travis Bradberry and Jean Graves, *Emotional Intenlligence 2.0* (TalentSmart, June 2009).

Jim Collins, *Good to Great: Why Some Companies Make the Leap … and Others Don't* (New York, HarperCollins Publishers, 2001).

Carmine Gallo, *The Apple Experience: Secrets to Building Insanely Great Customer Loyalty* (McGraw-Hill, 2012).

Jeffery Gitomer, *Customer Satisfaction Is Worthless, Customer Loyalty Is Priceless: How to Make Customers Love You, Keep Them Coming Back and Tell Everyone They Know* (Bard Press, 1998).

John C. Maxwell, *The 21 Irrefutable Laws of Leadership: Follow Them and People Will Follow You* (Thomas Nelson, 2007).

Mark Sanborn, *The Fred Factor* (DoubleDay, May 2004).

Simon Sinek, *Start with Why: How Great Leaders Inspire Everyone to Take Action* (Portfolio, 2009).

Gino Wickman and Mark C. Winters, *Rocket Fuel* (Dallas, Benbella Books, 2015).